Cool Rules

Focus on Contemporary Issues (FOCI) addresses the pressing problems, ideas and debates of the new millennium. Subjects are drawn from the arts, sciences and humanities, and are linked by the impact they have had or are having on contemporary culture. FOCI books are intended for an intelligent, alert audience with a general understanding of, and curiosity about, the intellectual debates shaping culture today. Instead of easing readers into a comfortable awareness of particular fields, these books are combative. They offer points of view, take sides and are written with passion.

SERIES EDITORS
Barrie Bullen and Peter Hamilton

Cool Rules

Anatomy of an Attitude

DICK POUNTAIN
AND DAVID ROBINS

REAKTION BOOKS

Published by Reaktion Books Ltd
33 Great Sutton Street
London EC1V 0DX, UK

www.reaktionbooks.co.uk

First published 2000
Transferred to digital printing 2009

Designed and typeset by Libanus Press
Printed and bound by Chicago University Press

British Library Cataloguing in Publishing Data
Pountain, Dick
    Cool rules : anatomy of an attitude
    1. Popular culture – Great Britain – History 2. Social influence
    3. Attitude (Psychology) – Great Britain 4. Great Britain – Social
    life and customs – 1945–
    I. Title II. Robins, David, 1944–
    306.4'0941

ISBN 978 1 86189 071 9

Contents

Introduction   7

1 What is Cool?   15

2 Out of Africa   34

3 A Whiter Shade of Cool   52

4 That's Cool Too . . .   71

5 Cool Cracks Up   94

6 The Look of Cool   114

7 Cool Relations   132

8 Cool Psyche   146

9 Cool Rules   160

References   183

Acknowledgements   188

Photographic Acknowledgements   189

Introduction

The idea for this book arose from personal experience of conflict between the musical tastes of different generations. As parents of teenage children we could not help but notice a revival of the use of the word *cool* as a term of approbation, but neither could we ignore the fact that it was being applied to very different objects – Stan Getz and Charles Mingus for the parents, Wu Tang Clan and Basement Jaxx for the children (this month).

Our starting point was to wonder what, if anything, there was in common between the concept of Cool as used by ourselves and by our children – clearly, our choice of music, haircut and clothes could not be the answer. Was there some core meaning that persisted from generation to generation, regardless of changes in musical and sartorial fashion? (Beyond, that is, the wearing of dark glasses, which are apparently timeless in their appeal.) What was clear was that for several generations young people have been absorbing, redefining and appearing to reject their parents' notion of Cool.

Our inquiry makes no claim to be a comprehensive social-scientific survey: it was more of an experiment, to see how far we could use this concept of Cool to explain the evolution of popular culture over the last 50 years, as well as to provide a set of directions for further research. We believe that for this purpose a work of popular social commentary is more appropriate than a rigorous academic treatise, given the breadth of the fields in which traces of Cool are to be found – from African history and jazz, through '60s cinema to '90s loft living.

As regards method, we have been quite eclectic, exploring many fields, from social psychology to cultural anthropology, in which we can claim no special expertise. As well as examining fragments of history, to compare the ways in which Cool has appeared among different generations, we have drawn on sociology and social psychology to explore the group-dynamic dimensions of Cool, psychology and psychoanalysis to examine the Cool personality and its relation to others, and literary analysis to see how Cool works in film and the written word. To some readers our perspective on Cool may bear a passing resemblance to postmodernist critics such as Fredric Jameson, particularly at those moments when we attempt to position Cool in relation to Modernism and place it at the heart of the consumerist ethic. However, we have adopted neither the language of postmodern criticism and textual analysis nor its underlying premises – indeed we have committed sundry sins against the strictures of postmodern methodology, not the least of which are historicism and psychologism. We plead guilty in advance to such methodological naivety, to believing that there is such a thing as history and that real people with minds live through it. If called to account, we can only plead that we were lead astray by reading brilliant scholars like Peter Gay, whose unashamed use of psychoanalytical concepts in the study of history makes more sense to us than most of the arid deconstruction currently in fashion.

We have, with a single exception, refrained from inventing any arcane new terminology. That exception is that throughout this book we have used the capitalized word *Cool* to refer to that underlying psychological stance or attitude which we are searching for, with its distinctive history and structure. We have done this in order to distinguish it from other uses of the word *cool* – for example the weaker (but related) use of 'cool' in popular speech to mean 'good', its traditional (and again, related) use as a synonym for 'nonchalant' or 'unflappable', or its use to describe the temperature at which white wine (or lager) should be drunk. If it helps, think of capitalized Cool as some Platonic (or better still Hegelian) essence of Cool.

At this point we should explain why we did not choose the almost synonymous term *hip* instead of *cool*. We were tempted, especially at the beginning of the project when the UK press appeared to be making Cool references ad nauseam. However, in the end we decided that 'cool' was a broader, as well as historically a longer-lived, term than 'hip'. Probably the most penetrating study of Hip is still Norman Mailer's 1957 essay *The White Negro*, which, despite its quaintly dated argot, politically incorrect racial terminology and now unfashionable emphasis on sexuality and psychoanalysis, grasps the essential motivation of the hipster (a term which Mailer almost owns) in a way that few other accounts have. In that essay Mailer identified Cool as an *attribute* of the hipster ... 'to be cool, to be in control of a situation because you have swung where the Square has not ...'[1] We chose the term precisely because it is not tied to that particular historical manifestation that was called Hip. We want to show that Cool is and has been an attribute of many more groups than the '50s hipster, and that, unlike Hip, Cool can be an attribute of objects as well as people.

We do not of course claim to have 'discovered' Cool. Scores of music and style journalists have been there already, fondling its contours and inventing new names for its various extremities – Girl Power, Middle Youth, New Lads etc. Diktats issued by the editors of style magazines on what is, or is not, deemed Cool this month may appear to be a trivial matter, but the profitability of large business sectors now depends on such pronouncements. This has led to a perception that Cool is merely a passing fad, and has deterred many serious commentators from analyzing the phenomenon. For example, a trawl of the Internet for references to 'cool' reveals that the word is most often used indiscriminately for effect, especially by fashion, style and rock journalists – *David Bowie: Out of the Cool* or *Mick Jagger: Primitive Cool* give the flavour. (A more accurate title for such hagiographies might have been *Millionaire Cool*.) A similar search for the word *cool* in academic databases yields references to essays on 'cyberpunk' and 'hypertext' in the field of cultural studies, but most of these refer in turn to *Cool Memories*, a collection of critical essays on contemporary culture by the French philosopher Jean Baudrillard. That title was adopted by Baudrillard's English translator, and the word is employed for its connotations of style, thoughtfulness, a certain joie de vivre – because it has a 'good sound'. There is no evidence in this collection of essays, or elsewhere in his oeuvre, that Baudrillard has interrogated or deconstructed Cool. For our own part we decline to reduce the phenomenon to merely another instance of 'oppositional cultural practices' involving 'cultural consumers', 'subverting musical hierarchies', 'transgressing media-generated gender roles' or 'celebrating cultural differences'. 'And all without the culture industries which have produced these things catching on', as Thomas Frank has acidly remarked.[2]

There have been a few empirical studies of the concept of Cool and we will be referring to these throughout. Significantly, all of them were published in the USA or Canada during the early '90s, a formative period in the latest manifestation of Cool. In *Cool Pose: The Dilemmas of Black Manhood in America* (1992), Richard Majors and Janet Mancini Billson examine Cool from an ethnic perspective, viewing it as a crucial component of the African-American male character. For Marcel Tadesi in *Cool: The Signs and Meanings of Adolescence* (1994), Cool is an age-specific phenomenon, defined as 'the central behavioural trait of teenagerhood (sic).'[3] In *American Cool: Constructing a Twentieth-Century Emotional Style* (1994), Peter Stearns seeks to place the subject in a broader historical context, seeing the rise of Cool as a gradual, century-long flight out of nineteenth-century sentimentalism. *American Cool* is the culmination of Stearns's epic study, which he calls The History of the Emotions in America, and which follows previous studies on jealousy and anger.

An invaluable recent study is Thomas Frank's *The Conquest of Cool* (1997), the first detailed analysis of the rise of Hip consumerism in the '60s and its transformation of US business culture. According to Frank, 'what happened in the sixties is that hip (or cool) became central to the way capitalism understood itself and explained itself to the public.'[4] Finally, *Bohemia: Digging the Roots of Cool* (1996), the memoirs of the novelist Herbert Gold, sheds light on how Cool became the studied attitude of American and European artistic bohemia during the '50s and '60s.

Although all these studies are authoritative in their own domains, those domains are rather restricted and seldom encroach on each other's territory – it feels as though they are writing about five different 'cools'. Tadesi fixes exclusively on the semiotics of teenage lifestyle and adolescent narcissism; for Stearns the concept is 'distinctly American' but he omits its African-American dimension, or its impact on political and artistic subcultures; Majors and Billson devote little space to the impact of black Cool on the wider US culture. We believe that we are the first to step back and observe the phenomenon as a whole. Our range of reference is of necessity wider, and our conclusions more far-reaching. So far as we know, this is the first book to establish Cool as a cultural category in its own right.

A New Mode of Individualism

Our own thesis may be briefly summarized this way. Cool appeared in the mainstream of Western culture barely 50 years ago, but we can trace similar phenomena right back to the ancient civilizations of West Africa, from where they may have been transported to the New World by the slave trade. There are also strikingly similar phenomena to be found in European culture, like the *sprezzatura* of Italian courtiers during the Renaissance, the famous reserve of the English aristocrat and the Romantic irony of nineteenth-century poets. Cool is by no means solely an American phenomenon, although its modern manifestation was incubated among black American jazz musicians during the first decades of the twentieth century, before being discovered by hard-boiled crime writers and Hollywood scriptwriters during the '30s and '40s, and finally injected into white youth culture during the '50s by Elvis Presley and rock 'n' roll. Thom Gunn's poem about the young Elvis, who 'turns revolt into a style', captures the combative nature of that original Cool:

> Whether he poses or is real, no cat
> Bothers to say: the pose held is a stance,
> Which, generation of the very chance
> It wars on, may be posture for combat.[5]

Cool has been a vital component of all youth subcultures from the '50s to the present day, although it has sometimes had to change its name (and even more frequently its costume) to confuse its parents. But we will show how this attitude, which originally expressed resistance to subjugation and humiliation, has been expropriated by the mass media and the advertising industry during the '80s and '90s, and used as the way into the hearts and wallets of young consumers. The meaning of Cool has changed profoundly in the decades since Gunn recognized it in the 'posture for combat' of a tiny minority of outsiders. It is now in the process of taking over the whole of popular culture, and if its conquest is not quite uncontested some of its competitors for the modern heart and mind – various nationalisms and religious fundamentalisms – are far from attractive. Cool could even prove to be the new mode of individualism, an adaptation to life in post-industrial consumer democracies, much as the Protestant work ethic that Max Weber described was a way of living the discipline of industrial societies. However, if that proves to be the case, then Cool still retains enough of its potently antisocial content to cause upsets for any politicians who dare to dabble with it as a potential vote-winner. Government health warnings notwithstanding, Cool is still in love with cigarettes, booze and drugs. It now admits women but it loves violence far more than it used to. It still loves the sharp clothes and haircuts, but has discovered a preference for winners over losers. It still loves the night, and flirts with living on the edge. If, as we believe, Cool is destined to become the dominant ethic among the younger generations of the whole developed world and billions of 'wannabes' in developing countries, then understanding it ought to be a matter of some urgency for educationalists and health agencies. That is, if we are to avoid debacles such as the now infamous British Health Council poster that showed a wasted young man ravaged by heroin. (It had to be withdrawn because young people sought copies as pin-ups for their bedroom walls.)

Polka dots may come and go, but shades will always be Cool. Bob Dylan *c*. 1963.

CHAPTER ONE

What is Cool?

In March 1999 the Levi Strauss company of San Francisco, the largest clothing brand in the world and purveyor of blue jeans to generations of cowboys and teenagers, announced that it would close half of its US plants and lay off 6,000 workers. The reason given was a slump in sales (Levi's market share halved between 1990 and 1998) but beneath that reason lies another – Levi's blue jeans are no longer Cool. The question of what is, and what is not, Cool is a matter not solely for schoolyard discussion but also for the boardrooms of all kinds of businesses, from soft drinks and snacks to clothes, cars and computers. Profits and jobs depend upon what may seem a trivial and juvenile distinction to many people.

Cool is rarely out of the news nowadays. One day we are told that UK teachers plan to 'challenge low aspiration among disaffected youth by promoting the perception that learning is cool', while next the Barbican Art Gallery in London is staging a retrospective of '60s photographs by David Bailey under the title *Birth of the Cool*. There is a resurgence of interest, accompanied by new biographies, of the beat generation writers Kerouac, Ginsberg and Burroughs. Cool even affects property prices –

15

a recent book by Mark Irving and Marcus Field chronicles the way in which Abstract Expressionists and other artists in New York City during the '50s and '60s colonized grimy lofts in old commercial premises as a form of resistance against Modernist urban redevelopment plans.' However, during the early '90s a dramatic shift occurred as imaginative property developers moved in on the loft market; 'From being zones of feisty individualism, lofts became about being rich, marketed as the places in which "movers and shakers" planned their next career spectacular . . . Suddenly inner-city living was cool.'[1]

Then there is the darker side of Cool. The US hip-hop culture seethes with violence, from the gunning down of artists Tupac Shakur and Biggie Smalls to the indictment of Puff Daddy for GBH and assault against his video producer. Columbine High School in Denver, Colorado – where in April 1999 two 'goths' massacred 25 of their fellow students – was described in the media as divided into four or five sub-cultures, each believing themselves Cooler than the rest, while the killers themselves allegedly consumed 'industrial quantities' of drugs. Even the 1999 Kosovo crisis yielded Cool connections: press photographs showed Serbian paramilitaries (and their opposite numbers in the Kosovo Liberation Army) sporting tattoos, bandannas and T-shirts bearing Hell's Angels insignia, plus the ultimate style accessory, a Kalashnikov assault rifle. While Nato bombs fell on Belgrade, the city's young people attended rock concerts, hiding in dance clubs rather than bomb shelters and smoking Albanian-grown weed. It is said that during the 1996 siege of Sarajevo, Belgrade clubbers would drive out after a night at the disco to take pot shots at the hapless citizens from the surrounding hills. Meanwhile the Western world is witnessing an epidemic of heroin and cocaine abuse (the two Coolest drugs of all).

What all these references, and many more, suggest is that Cool is not merely a passing fad but is becoming a universal phenomenon that has an important influence on all our institutions, from the media and

Confounded by Cool. A 1988 British health-education poster showing a young man ravaged by heroin addiction had to be withdrawn because young people sought copies to hang in their bedrooms.

education to the real estate market and the economy itself (both legal and underground). It is only a slight exaggeration to say that movements in Cool are reported with the same gravity that was once reserved for the gold standard.

A Moving Target

So what exactly is Cool? That is a difficult question to answer at several levels. Firstly there arises the question of its ontological status: what kind of an entity is Cool? Is it a philosophy, a sensibility, a religion, an ideology, a personality type, a behaviour pattern, an attitude, a zeitgeist, a worldview? We shall not concern ourselves too deeply with this question here, leaving that pleasure for others. Rather we intend to take an unfashionably naive approach by simply accepting Cool as a phenomenon that we can recognize when we see it, from its effects in human behaviour and cultural artefacts – in speech and dance, films and television shows, books and magazines, music, clothes, paintings, cars, computers or motorcycles. It doesn't take too much investigation to understand that Cool is not something that inheres in these artefacts themselves, but rather in people's attitude to them. Levi Strauss found out the hard way that Cool is not an intrinsic property woven into the blue denim of its jeans: it was the way that their wearers perceived Levi's that made them Cool, and within a few years that perception would be imperceptibly seduced away by Calvin Klein and Tommy Hilfiger.

If Cool is inherent in people rather than objects, then what is seen as Cool will change from place to place, from time to time, from generation to generation. Danny Boyle's 1996 film *Trainspotting*.

Around the time of the plant closures Levi Strauss's vice-president of marketing was reported as saying that 'What kids want is to be acceptable to their peers' (reported by Hal Espen in *The New York Times*), but that is only half the answer, and is profoundly symptomatic of how far wrong Levi Strauss had gone. Kids want simultaneously to be acceptable to their peers *and* scandalous to their parents. What originally made Levi's Cool in the '50s was that they were garments associated with the working classes – the term 'blue-collar' is a reference to denim work-shirts. In the '50s and '60s, for a middle-class kid to wear blue denim rather than grey flannel was an act of symbolic rebellion. But in the '90s those sartorial rebels are parents and still wearing their Levi's, so their own children must find something different to express their rebellion. In the UK this was made hilariously explicit when a 1998 consumer survey discovered that Jeremy Clarkson, an aggressively middle-class (and blue-jeans-wearing) presenter of *Top Gear*, a television programme about cars, was almost single-handedly responsible for making denim Uncool to the under-thirties.

Here then is a basis for a rough working definition of Cool that may serve until more of its properties are uncovered in later chapters. Cool is an oppositional attitude adopted by individuals or small groups to express defiance to authority – whether that of the parent, the teacher, the police, the boss or the prison warden. Put more succinctly, we see Cool as a *permanent* state of *private* rebellion. *Permanent* because Cool is not just some 'phase that you go through', something that you 'grow out of', but rather something that if once attained remains for life; *private* because Cool is not a collective political response but a stance of individual defiance, which does not announce itself in strident slogans but conceals its rebellion behind a mask of ironic impassivity. This attitude is in the process of becoming the dominant type of relation between people in Western societies, a new secular virtue. No-one wants to be good any more, they want to be Cool, and this desire is no longer

As Cool likes to live dangerously, government health warnings about smoking are likely to prove counter-productive. Humphrey Bogart (1899–1957).

confined to teenagers but is to be found in a sizeable minority even of the over-50s who were permanently affected by the '60s counter-culture.

This brings us to a second difficulty in defining Cool, namely its mutability. If Cool is not inherent in objects but in people, then what is seen as Cool will change from place to place, from time to time and from generation to generation. Those marketing managers at Levi Strauss desperately trying to 'crack the code of cool' know that their jeans were granted Cool status by an accident of history, and advertising alone cannot recapture it for them.

In any epoch, although Cool will have a particularly powerful meaning for teenagers, as an antidote to their ever-present fear of being embarrassed, being Cool forms part of a risky series of negotiations about becoming an individual while still being accepted into a group – it's about both individuality and belonging, and the tension between the two. Once acquired, Cool does not wear off quickly, and since in its modern form it appeared in the '50s, there are now at least four generations alive who have their own – often seriously clashing – definitions of what is Cool. Recent studies of under-30 drug users reveal that a significant number have parents who first experimented with drugs in the '60s and '70s (when they were Cool themselves) and who are now in a quandary about what to tell their children. Each succeeding generation feels that 'real' Cool is something pure and existential known only to them – it was founded in *their* time, in the jazz clubs of the '50s, or the hippy festivals of the '60s, or the punk explosion of the '70s. One component of Cool is certainly a retarded adolescence, inspired in part by a morbid fear of ageing – anyone who has been to a party where 50-somethings get down to the strains of 'Get Off of My Cloud' have had a glimpse of the *danse macabre.*

On the other hand, Cool is equally about teenagers behaving with precocious maturity (especially about sex and political cynicism), and older hipsters are discovering that the behaviour they employed as provocation in the '60s is now accepted as everyday routine: city streets, cafés, movie theatres and clubs thronged with exuberant youth for whom wearing hair long or sporting a nose ring is considered quite a mild social statement (it's easy to forget that in 'swinging London' in the '60s the burger joint was the only place open after 10.30pm).

Distinctive clothes and haircuts have always been key signifiers of Cool, but that doesn't make it purely a matter of fashion. Fashion is the court in which Cool displays itself, but it penetrates deeper than that, down into 'that within which passeth show' as Hamlet (one of the first Cool heroes of literature) would have it. Cool is not simply emotional shallowness, lack of passion or enthusiasm, as it is sometimes parodied. Cool's real work is done inside: inside the seventeen-year-old lad who spends his money on deodorants and Tommy Hilfiger and likes what he sees in the mirror (while fighting down his internal panic that his true feelings might rise up to overwhelm him); and equally inside the successful, fashionable young woman who lives in thrall to an abusive man. Many modern egos are held together by the powerful spiritual adhesive that is Cool. A carefully cultivated Cool pose can keep the lid on the most intense feelings and violent emotions. In the street culture of America's inner cities, as glorified in gangsta rap, Cool is considered such an important source of respect that people will commit homicide in order to maintain it.

It's tempting to see Cool as a primarily male phenomenon, an exaggeration of the young male's tendency toward peacock display and emotional detachment, but it is more complicated than that. There is a sense in which many of the original Cool role models of the '50s – James Dean, Frank Sinatra, Marlon Brando and Montgomery Clift – represented a new feminization of traditional masculine images and a break with orthodox macho constructs of the desirable male. The contribution of gay culture (both underground and 'out') to the development of Cool is a story that has yet to be told. Also in film and popular music there is a long and strong tradition of Cool female role models, from Garbo, Stanwyck, Dietrich and Bacall, through Billie Holiday, to Nico and Chrissie Hynde. As the new secular virtue, Cool now inspires women as much as it does men, from smart television executives to single parents living in housing developments.

Another misconception about Cool, and one that is equally prevalent among both champions of high culture and their leftist detractors, is that it represents nothing more than US cultural imperialism: that it is simply American popular culture exported around the world. It is certainly true that Cool in its present form has roots in pre-war American black culture and was co-opted and disseminated by Hollywood movies and rock music. However, we shall demonstrate that similar phenomena have emerged in many different countries and over many centuries, and that even in the post-war decades Cool has been significantly shaped by European influences, not least by British popular music and humour.

Cool is a rebellious attitude, an expression of a belief that the mainstream mores of your society have no legitimacy and do not apply to you. It's a self-contained and individualistic attitude, although it places high value on friendship within a tightly defined peer group – indeed it strives to displace traditional family ties, which are too intimate and intrusive to allow sufficient space for self-invention. Cool is profoundly hedonistic but often to such a self-destructive degree that it flirts with death: by accident, suicide or some ambivalent admixture of the two (for example, a motorcycle crash or auto-erotic strangulation). Cool was once an attitude fostered by rebels and underdogs – slaves, prisoners, political dissidents – for whom open rebellion invited punishment, so it hid its defiance behind a wall of ironic detachment, distancing itself from the source of authority rather than directly confronting it. In the '50s this attitude was widely adopted by artists and intellectuals who thereby aided its infiltration into popular culture, with the result that today it is becoming the dominant attitude, even (or perhaps especially) among the rich and privileged who can wield it as merely the latest in a long line of weapons with which to put down their 'social inferiors'. Contemporary Cool is equally at home in the tenement basement and the million-dollar loft conversion. At its most extreme, Cool can even be turned into a manipulative strategy for separating people from their families and encouraging dependency: 'control freaks' such as Charles Manson, David Khoresh of the Branch Dravidians (of Waco notoriety), the Reverend Jim Jones and gurus like the Bagwhan Shri Rajneesh have all deployed Cool as an aspect of their manipulative personas.

The New Arbiters of Cool

If Cool is the new virtue, then the worst sin you can commit against it is to be 'judgemental', that is, to make disparaging value judgements about someone else's lifestyle. The next worst sin is to do precisely what we are doing here, namely to attempt to define and analyze Cool. There is a glaring contradiction here, because Cool itself is intrinsically judgemental and exclusive: it can ultimately define itself only by excluding what is Uncool. Moreover the taboo against reflecting on the nature of Cool does not inhibit our mass media from obsessive discussions about what is or is not Cool, countless interviews that 'rediscover' Cool pioneers from the *demi-monde* and endless top-ten lists. Behind this discourse , however, lies a more pertinent question, namely 'Who will decide what is Cool?' For whoever decides wields great economic power.

Newspaper editors and their marketing directors are unashamedly dangling Cool as bait for the elusive young adult market. In the UK few readers can have failed to notice the extraordinary transformation that in recent years has overtaken that Great British Institution, the serious newspaper: *The Times, The Telegraph, The Observer, The Independent* and *The Guardian* have become virtually unrecognizable. As television has usurped their role as prime transmitters of news events, these 'serious' newspapers now sell lifestyle and opinion, recruiting hordes of columnists and editors from the style and fashion press to provide 'credible' coverage of the triumphal progress of Cool. A similar trend is discernible in television programming itself, to the extent that one media chief executive of the '90s (known to colleagues as the 'King of Cool') was reputed to commission programmes solely on the basis of whether they would project a suitably Hip image for his station. The evidence so far is that this strategy is failing to halt declines in newspaper circulation and viewing figures.

The election of the New Labour Government in 1997 sparked off a battle between these newspaper columnists to either support or trash a precariously concocted notion of 'Cool Britannia', which was fought by incorporating the greatest number of puns on Cool into their headlines. One newspaper even voted Cool its 'Word of the Year'. Glossy magazines splashed the word across their covers to exploit its 'feel-good' effect, flaunting membership of the in-crowd for just £2.50. A few more thoughtful commentators fought a desperate rearguard action. A British television critic, Desmond Christy (*The Guardian*, 3 July 1997), complained ironically that 'you can't really get a job in the media any more if you don't use the word "cool" as your response to most questions and situations.[2] A few examples: "What did you think of last night's X-Files?" Response: "Cool." "I voted New Labour." Response: "Cool." You soon get the hang of it and it saves you from ever being short of something to say.' *The Independent on Sunday* ran a fatuous feature entitled 'A Guide to What's Really Cool' which attacked opponents of Cool Britannia: 'Of course Cool is important', it babbled. 'Cool is the summation of all we aspire to. Cool is not an image, a way of looking, talking or doing. It is a way of being.' This provoked *The Guardian* to reply with an article entitled 'The Myth of Cool', opining that Cool was a marketing conspiracy dreamed up by the UK record industry in cahoots with a certain

American ice-cream manufacturer. Amusing as these journalistic contortions may have been, they are less than helpful in understanding what Cool actually stands for.

The Cool Personality

We will argue that Cool is an attitude or personality type that has emerged in many different societies, during different historical epochs, and which has served different social functions, but is nevertheless recognizable in all its manifestations as a particular combination of three core personality traits, namely narcissism, ironic detachment and hedonism.

Narcissism means an exaggerated admiration for oneself, particularly for personal appearance, which gives rise to the feeling that the world revolves around you and shares your moods. At its most positive such narcissism is a healthy celebration of the self, while even in its more negative manifestations it can be an effective adaptation to any oppressive circumstances that sap self-esteem. Such circumstances would appear to include not only the obvious experience of poverty, political repression and tyranny but even life in the celebrity-worshipping consumer democracies of the developed world. Of course to any puritan culture, narcissism appears as the sin of vanity.

Ironic detachment is a stratagem for concealing one's feelings by suggesting their opposite, for example feigning boredom in the face of danger, or amusement in the face of insult. Philosophers distinguish several types of irony, including Socratic irony, which involves saying less than one really means to lull an opponent into false security, while actually delivering a telling blow to his argument, and Romantic irony, a profound scepticism which questions the validity of everything (as exemplified in the aphorisms of Nietzsche). Cool irony partakes of both these meanings, making it a verbal weapon equally effective in aggression or defence, and crucial to the maintenance of a protective Cool persona. Irony allows one to give deep offence while ostensibly remaining civil, as in the black American tradition of 'shucking' speech used to address white authority figures, which offers a subservience so exaggerated that it becomes insolent. Jewish humour has a similar tradition of defensive-aggressive irony, and it was '60s comics such as Mort Sahl and Lenny Bruce, coming out of this tradition, who forged a new strain of 'sick humour', for example by deliberately using racial epithets as a way of defusing their power to hurt. This type of ironic humour now so suffuses modern Cool that displays of simple sincerity have become almost

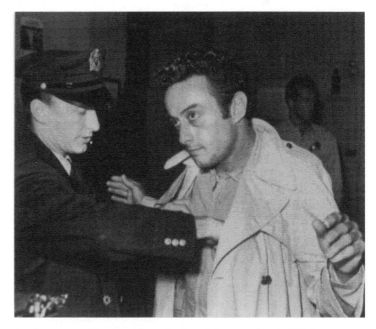

A policeman searching Lenny Bruce for drugs in San Francisco in 1961. Bruce forged the new strain of 'sick' ironic humour by deliberately employing racial epithets to defuse their power to hurt. This approach so suffuses contemporary Cool that displays of simple sincerity have become almost impossibly uncool.

impossibly Uncool – Quentin Tarantino can make mopping splattered brains off a car seat seem genuinely funny.

Hedonism requires less explanation, except perhaps to point out that Cool hedonism tends toward the worldly, adventurous and even orgiastic rather than the pleasant. At its lightest, Cool hedonism is that pursuit of happiness enshrined in the American Constitution and described so well by de Tocqueville as 'a love of physical gratification, the notion of bettering one's condition, the excitement of competition, the charm of anticipated success'. However, long before Freud, artists from Shakespeare to Balzac had understood that the pursuit of pleasure is seldom so uncomplicated – for the Byrons, Billie Holidays, Charlie Parkers and Hunter S. Thompsons of this world, the 'charm of anticipated success' would seem to be overshadowed by other, darker motivations.

We will try to establish three chief arguments about this combination of personality traits that we call Cool: that it has sufficient coherence to be recognizable as a 'syndrome' that is transmissible via culture and that has a traceable history (although we will do no more than sketch that history); that it is at odds with both European and American Puritan traditions; and that it has until recently appeared in those societies as a form of social deviance and rebellion, but that it is now losing this rebellious status and becoming the dominant ethic of late consumer capitalism. We will argue that Cool has mutated from a religious ethic that served to curb the aggression of young men in warrior societies, to a defence mechanism against the degradation of slavery, a form of rebellion against the conformity of industrial capitalism, and, more recently, a mechanism for coping with the competitive pressure of post-industrial consumer capitalism.

This last point brings us up against one of the central paradoxes of Cool, namely that while at one level it appears to be the antithesis of competition – a nonchalant, unruffled refusal to play by the man's rules – this is in fact a shallow pose that conceals ferociously competitive instincts. This competitive aspect of Cool is at its most obvious in the arena of sexual conquest, and only slightly less so in sartorial matters, which is a theme we shall revisit at several points in the book. If any reader doubts the reality of this paradox or has trouble encompassing its extremity, they might consider a particular paradigm case – that Coolest of all games, poker, which consists of little more than a number of people using the medium of a deck of cards to pit their Cools against one another, with the intention of financial and psychological conquest.

What we will *not* be doing here is presenting Cool as an ideology with any particular political content; on the contrary, Cool has attached itself at various times to a bewildering variety of causes and creeds, from cowboy machismo to animal rights, from pacifism to terrorism and from free-market enthusiasm to anti-capitalist anarchism. Behind such diverse manifestations, it is still possible to identify the Cool ethic and aesthetic at work. Take a seemingly trivial gesture like wearing sunglasses after the sun has gone down. Whether the wearer is a movie star, a rock singer, an eighteen-year-old on the prowl in Ibiza, an urban guerilla or a Latin American dictator, the gesture carries the same connotations of detachment and narcissism.

The C Word

A great source of confusion in understanding Cool is the word itself, which already has several closely related metaphorical usages, derived from its physical meaning of low temperature. For example, *The Oxford English Dictionary* offers this definition:

> Cool: to lose the heat of excitement or passion, to become less zealous or ardent. Not affected by passion or emotion, unexcited, deliberate, calm.

... while Jonathon Green in his *Dictionary of Slang* (1998) gives its vernacular usages as:

> Cool: late nineteenth century+: good or fine or pleasing; twentieth century: calm, self-possessed, aware and sophisticated; 1940+: fashionable, chic or with it.[3]

These meanings accurately describe an important aspect of the Cool attitude, but at the same time they conceal its underlying transgressive elements, the ironic and defiant character that distinguishes it from many previous versions of nonchalance and savoir-faire. A correspondent to the letters pages of *The London Evening Standard* (April 1999) claimed that this limited sense of the word dates back at least as far as the mid-nineteenth century, and was used by Dickens in 1836 in *Pickwick Papers*: '[the coachman] pulls out his handkerchief, and wipes his forehead; partly because he has a habit of doing it, and partly because it's as well to show the passengers how cool he is, and what an easy thing it is to drive a four-in-hand, when you've had as much practice as he has.' This prompted another correspondent to retort with an example of its use in a more ironic sense by Chaucer: 'thou thinkest in thy wit that is full cole / That he nys but a verray propre fole.'

'Cool' in its meaning of 'good', 'fine' or 'fashionable' is now used as a universal term of approval among the young in North America and the UK (as well as in many non-English-speaking countries), right from children in primary school playgrounds up to college-age adults. A language-use survey conducted among late adolescent junior college students in the USA gave 'cool' a 91.57% use and recognition rating, concluding that the word is a key element of a meta-code that cuts across all the many subspecies of teenage argot. Does this then imply that 'cool' is a precise synonym for 'good' and has no deeper content? On the contrary, 'cool' always carries an extra, often barely perceived, connotation: describing something (a record, a movie, a soft drink) as 'cool' rather than 'swell' or 'dandy' makes the statement, in however small a way, that the person who utters it is Cool and not a nerd or a conformist. Of course the nine-year-old in primary school will not understand such connotations at first, but they will gradually absorb precisely what it is that makes some things Cool and others not in the eyes of their peers, so that merely using the word forms part of an unofficial, alternative process of socialization. Peter Stearns had grasped this meaning when he said that the use of 'cool' acts as 'an emotional mantle, sheltering the whole personality from embarrassing excess . . . using the word is part of the process of conveying the right impression'.[4]

The implication is that in many contexts 'cool' actually means the precise opposite of 'good'. If someone says 'It's cool to do coke' they don't mean that it's *good* citizenship to take cocaine, or *good* for your health to take cocaine: they mean it is intensely pleasurable to take cocaine, and that the fact that it's illegal makes taking cocaine more exciting and makes them Cooler in the eyes of their peers. This sort of ironic inversion of values underlies many other Cool-slang terms like the use of 'wicked' or traditionally unclean terms like 'shit' and 'funky' as terms of approval. Among currently fashionable expressions, 'Yeah, right . . .' is intended to express its exact opposite 'No, wrong,' while 'Whatever . . .' as an expression of acquiescence conveys the speaker's total detachment from the outcome of the decision in question – 'That's fine by me!' would express an Uncool degree of enthusiasm. Stearns offers a nice anecdote to illustrate the consequences of such ironic reversals: 'A university student writes in an examination that Columbus received a hearty welcome on his return to Spain; when asked why he made such an egregious historical error, he points to the textbook which states quite clearly that the explorer had received "a cool reception".'[5]

In the USA controversy has surrounded the subcultural origins of the word *cool* rather than its etymology. Some have claimed the expression originated in the jazz club scene of the '30s: 'When the air of the smoke-filled nightclubs of that era became unbreathable, windows and doors were opened to allow some "cool air" in . . . By analogy, the slow and smooth jazz style that was typical of that late-night scene came to be called "cool". Cool was subsequently extended to describe any physically attractive male jazz musician, or aficionado who patronized such clubs.'[6] This has the slightly bogus feel of a 'myth of origins', but what is certainly true is that music and sex played a major part in the derivation of Cool, as in the blues lyric 'Some like their man hot, but I like him cool.' In fact the word *cool* became attached to one particular style of jazz in the late '40s and '50s, compounding a confusion between the musical style and the attitude (which was exhibited by far more jazz musicians than ever played the style). Besides, the finger-clicking teenagers of *West Side Story* probably brought the word into the consciousness of more white, middle-class Americans than jazz ever did. Among the '60s hippies 'cool' took on a slightly narrower meaning – closer to its traditional implication of nonchalance – of a calming down to better deal with a problem, which has metamorphosed into the current usage 'to chill'. However, it was the hip-hop culture of the '80s and '90s that restored to 'cool' (or 'kool') those transgressive and defiant connotations that it still bears for many teenagers today. In the next few chapters we will investigate where this concept of Cool came from, why it finds such a resonance in modern society, and how it operates at the psychological level.

Whichever way you spell it, it's as well to remember that the word *cool* is not merely another way of saying 'good'. It comes with baggage – an alternative set of values which are often profoundly in conflict with official values. For example it is not very smart for a political party to carelessly promote Cool Britannia when it is also committed to a policy of reducing drug abuse. Creative directors in advertising have by now an almost perfect understanding of the power of Cool to sell products to young people, profound enough that they seldom need to brandish the raw word itself (which could be construed as rather Uncool). Indeed they have become so expert at suggesting the attitude through surrealistic imagery and veiled drug references that many television advertisements are now all but incomprehensible to anyone over 30. The agencies understand that to be perceived as Cool demands precisely such a conspiratorial pact with their target viewers, and it is highly significant that Levi Strauss has regained its lost ground with the cryptic but hugely popular 'Flat Eric' advertising campaign, featuring a battered old car (take that Jeremy Clarkson), no words and a stuffed toy with attitude.

CHAPTER TWO

Out of Africa

Although the concept of Cool only took on the full meaning we are ascribing to it during the twentieth century, what appear to be closely related ideas and attitudes may be found throughout history and all over the world. Attitudes that had much in common with modern Cool were detectable within many artistic and cultural movements, in many countries, from German Romanticism, through Dada and Surrealism, to New York Abstract Expressionism. As for modern popular music and cinema, we will argue that Cool is one of their guiding principles, and that they serve to propagate it around the world. However, the undeniable historical fact that so much of twentieth-century popular culture originated from the USA has lead some commentators to conclude that Cool is an entirely American phenomenon, and that its spread to other countries then has to be explained as an example of US cultural imperialism. To Peter Stearns, the author of *American Cool* (1994), for example, 'the concept is distinctly American. From Kool cigarettes and the Snoopy cartoon's Joe Cool, the idea of cool, in its many manifestations, has seized a central place in the American imagination.'[1] But one might want to insert here 'the white American imagination', for whether by accident or by design Stearns pretty well ignores all the evidence that the twentieth-century variant of Cool originated among black Americans. In fact it is possible to trace similar attitudes in the ancient civilizations of West Africa, and modern Cool may represent the survival and adaptation of such attitudes as transported to America and Europe by the slave trade.

There is evidence to support this thesis in the pioneering research of the art historian Robert Farris Thompson. In his seminal studies

An Akan terracotta head from Ghana. In Africa, the metaphor of coolness goes well beyond self-control and nonchalance; it is a positive attribute which combines notions of composure, silence, vitality, healing and social purification.

African Art in Motion (1979) and *Flash of the Spirit* (1984), he suggests that the concept of *itutu*, which he translates as 'cool', is a central concept in the animistic religions of the Yoruba and Ibo civilizations of West Africa who built the ancient city-states of Ife-Ife and Benin. Thompson relates how citizens of the Yoruba city-states embraced a religious philosophy that valued composure or cool as one of its three main pillars, the other two being command (*ashe*) and character (*iwa*). In *African Art in Motion*, Thompson states that

> Cool is the overarching value that binds the concepts together
> ... the criterion of coolness seems to unite and animate all

the other canons ... Cool philosophy is a strong intellectual attitude, affecting incredibly diverse provinces of artistic happening, yet leavened with humour and a sense of play. It is an all-important mediating process, accounting for similarities in art and vision in many tropical African societies. It is a matrix from which stem ideas about being generous.[2]

Cool or *itutu* contained meanings of conciliation and gentleness of character, the ability to defuse fights and disputes, of generosity and grace. It was associated, but not identified entirely, with physical beauty. In *Flash of the Spirit*, Thompson quotes a Yoruba elder as saying, 'beauty is a part of coolness but beauty does not have the force that character has. Beauty comes to an end. Character is forever.' Or again, a Yoruba poem:

A man may be very, very handsome
Handsome as a fish within the water
But if he has no character
He is no more than a wooden doll.[3]

The reference to water here is typical because to the Yoruba coolness retained its physical connotation of temperature – it is hardly surprising that on a continent where drought represents a constant threat to survival, coolness should be numbered among the supreme virtues. *Itutu* was also ritually associated with the colour blue, and one may speculate whether this has anything to do with singing 'the blues', or with blue denim becoming the Cool garb of '50s and '60s America. When a Yoruba became possessed by the spirit of one of their deities, others could recognize his condition because his face froze into a mask – the mask of Cool. In fact some of the most stereotypical images of African society convey aspects of this philosophy: for example the fanning of chieftains with palm fronds was both to cool them physically and to pay homage to their spiritual Cool.

A Kamajor fighter wearing a traditional hunting mask during the 1997 Sierra Leone civil war. Such masks can convey ferocity and a 'cool face' in the presence of danger simultaneously.

This centrality of coolness in African religions is by no means confined to West Africa. Among the Bantu-speaking peoples of southern Africa, Coolness symbolizes 'what is good, normal and desirable' in society, so that communication with ancestral spirits for instance is only possible when people are sufficiently 'cool' – that is, neither angry nor spiteful.[4] There is a custom among the Tsonga and other African peoples of presenting their newborn infants to the moon, which is supposed to act as a cooling agent to counter the 'heat' of the screaming infant (a custom referred to by Alex Haley in his best-selling novel, *Roots*, as surviving in his own African-American family).

In both Yoruba and other African societies, political power was intimately associated with control over your own body, expressed through the medium of ritual and particularly of dance. So a theory to explain how Yoruba Cool survived and transformed itself in America might run along these lines. Once transported to America, Africans were forced to surrender their physical integrity and work as plantation slaves, but perhaps they felt that they could protect some part of their spiritual integrity by clinging to Cool, which afforded them a symbolic territory beyond the jurisdiction of their white owners – a secret, shared, black (and at that time almost exclusively male) discourse. All that their white owners were allowed to see were caricatures of subservience, heavy with irony, behind a Cool mask that concealed the contempt and rage that the slaves felt, the frank expression of which would have brought down harsh physical punishment.

Thompson demonstrates that core ideas from African religions travelled with the slaves to Latin America, the Caribbean and the Southern USA and remain visible today in the various so-called 'voodoo' cults. There are other aspects of African culture that survived too, among them the love of colourful textiles and clothing, and a distinctive easy gait, rolling from the hip. That gait has to be learned in childhood, and Thompson recounts how a Yoruba mother told her child, 'the way you walk signals your station in life.' In the '60s the sociologist Gerald Suttles noted how in the inner city neighbourhoods of Chicago 'Negro boys . . . have a "cool" way of walking in which the upper trunk and pelvis rock fore and aft while the head remains stable with the eyes looking straight ahead. The . . . walk is quite slow, and the Negroes take it as a way of strutting or showing off.'[5]

In their book *Cool Pose*, a study of the dilemmas of black manhood in America, Richard Majors and Janet Mancini Billson build on Thompson's arguments, even suggesting that cool philosophy may have been at work in Africa as early as 3000–2000 BC.[6] The authors argue persuasively that this same Cool was adapted and evolved by slave and ex-slave communities as a means of defending their pride and self-esteem in the face of continued racial discrimination and persecution. Like Thompson, Majors and Mancini Billson point to the survival of recognizably African fetish objects in the Southern USA, such as the Mojo Tooth and John the Conqueroo, and although their original meaning is lost to us, these talismans seem quite familiar after decades of hearing R&B bands perform Muddy Waters's 'Got My Mojo Working'. Other historians of slavery provide support for the argument that amid the horrors of enslavement, Africans managed to preserve a surprising degree of cultural autonomy, as expressed in the continuation of African patterns of behaviour. Herskowits (1941), for example, has argued that a great deal of African culture survived and persisted among the descendants of slaves – music, dance, styles of humour and modes of address – while in a more recent study, Ira Berlin shows that although the contours of slave life might have shifted, 'the beliefs, attitudes and activities that slaves nurtured among themselves always had an "oppositional content" even if concealed in the mimicry of dance or later in the metaphors of a folk tale.'[7]

It would be foolish to claim that whenever a child anywhere uses the word *cool* they are pledging allegiance to an ancient African philosophy, and that is not our contention. What we *are* claiming is that the attitude underlying the widespread use of the word among the young can be traced back to American culture, both black and white, and that this in turn has African roots, although in the intervening centuries it has become modified, added to and subtracted from in a million subtle ways. We cannot yet claim to have proved this thesis (perhaps others will take up that pursuit) and we are also aware of the profound controversy that currently surrounds all discussion of the effects of slavery on African-American life. The sociologist Orlando Patterson, for example, believes that slave property relations prevented the formation of genuine black families (or indeed any form of natural human bonding) in essence because 'husband', 'wife' and children all belonged to the slave owner rather than to each other. Patterson claims that this is the cause of 'the cool-pose culture' which he sees as an entirely negative inheritance of 'immorality and irresponsible behaviour' between men and women. Patterson is surely right to the extent that if the original African meaning of Cool survived slavery, it was greatly transformed by that brutal experience.[8]

The black consciousness movement has been arguing along such lines since the '60s, but often in a highly confrontational way, and often failing to distinguish between Cool or 'hip' and other attributes that it regards as proof of cultural superiority. African-American writers like Langston Hughes and Richard Wright were certainly aware of the unique role of Cool as early as the '50s and described it eloquently: 'There is in the African a latent lyricism which tends to express itself in movement, so that every gesture, every attitude of the body takes on a special significance which belongs to a language of which I caught only a few words.'[9] Or take these sardonic couplets from Hughes:

> I play it cool
> And dig all jive,

That's the reason

I stay alive

My motto as I live and learn

is: Dig and be dug in return [10]

In Africa Cool belonged to the realm of the sacred, but once transported to America it evolved into a new kind of passive resistance to
the work ethic through personal style. The Cool aesthetic was honed
during the early part of the twentieth century by those descendants
of Africans (together with some pioneering white colleagues) who played
jazz and blues, and who deployed Cool as a body armour against the
discrimination, patronization and neglect they experienced from the
mostly white-owned entertainment business. Ralph Ellison's *Invisible
Man* (1952) is a convincing depiction of the way that adopting this
early version of Cool made black people 'invisible' to most whites. It will

'I play it cool / And dig all jive' –
Langston Hughes, from *Motto*
(1938). Winold Reiss's pastel
portrait of Hughes (1925).

require a major effort of scholarship to trace the precise details of how this evolution occurred: how African Cool, once transplanted to the Americas, mutated and grew, inspiring early blues and jazz, then the Harlem Renaissance of the '20s, and finally becoming visible to whites via the urban crime folk tales of Dashiell Hammett, Raymond Chandler and the film noir genre. But one thing is clear – by the '50s whites wanted to be Cool too. And to quote Farris Thompson again: 'From there to bopping and hiphopping, rapping, and all the future ways that young men, white as well as black now, will look smart, publicly assert their strength of self, and rap their way to manhood . . . this image would seem indelible . . . resistant to destruction by Western materialist forces'.[11]

Blues Fell This Morning

Those parts of America in which the slaves found themselves were, with the notable exception of New Orleans, environments ruled by a sternly puritanical form of Protestant Christianity that could hardly have differed more from African religions. The slaves had no written language; their social organizations were deliberately disrupted by separating members of the same tribe; their sexual mores were brutally violated by breeding them like livestock; and any attempt to gain an education was punished.

How is it possible that under such appalling conditions a people could maintain any sort of culture at all, let alone communicate this to future generations? Yet they did, by inventing a new musical form called the blues, expressed in the language of their tormentors, English. Richard Wright, in his moving introduction to Paul Oliver's seminal work on blues lyrics, *The Blues Fell This Morning* (1960), put it like this: 'In a vocabulary terser than Basic English, shorn of all hyperbole, purged of all metaphysical implications, wedded to a frankly atheistic vision of life, and excluding almost all references to nature and her various moods, they sang:

> Whistle keeps on blowin' an' I got my debts to pay,
> I've got a mind to leave my baby an' I've got a mind to stay.[12]

The blues were by no means the only form of expression used by the slaves. Some of the more 'fortunate' slaves, mainly those who performed domestic duties and lived closest to the Big House, were converted to Christianity and evolved their own ebullient forms of Christian worship that combined frankly African musical elements with Christian concepts of sin and salvation. This gospel music defined itself in stern contradiction to the 'devil songs' of the blues, which were sung and appreciated by the lowest elements; the ditch diggers, the convicts, the migrant labourers, the pimps and the prostitutes. Wright is quick to pick up on this difference between the transcendental hopes expressed by gospel, and the atheistic, 'down and dirty' realism of the blues:

> The most striking feature of these songs [i.e. the blues] is that a submerged theme of guilt, psychological in nature, seems to run through them. Could this guilt have stemmed from the burden of renounced rebellious impulses? There is a certain degree of passivity, almost masochistic in quality and seemingly allied to sex in origin, that appears as part of the meaning of the blues. Could this emotional stance have been derived from a protracted inability to act, of a fear of acting?[13]

Modern forms of Cool have inherited precisely the ambiguous sensibility that Wright identified here, and we will see again and again a 'driven' quality that lies beneath Cool hedonism. Nihilism wrestles against guilt and a fear of retribution (a retribution to which that same nihilism denies any plausible agent) leading to an attempt to simultaneously rush toward and fly from self-destruction. You can see this modernized Manichean heresy at work behind The Rolling Stones's flirtations with satanic imagery in 'Sympathy for the Devil'; in virtually all of the iconography of Heavy Metal rock; in Robert de Niro's anguished characterization of Travis Bickle in Martin Scorsese's film *Taxi Driver*; or slyly mocked in Samuel L. Jackson's 'Ezekiel' rant in Quentin Tarantino's *Pulp Fiction.*

Greil Marcus detected the same phenomenon in his essay on Robert Johnson in the seminal collection of music essays *Mystery Train* (1974), where he explicitly links the tortured sexuality of Johnson's most

'Me and the devil was walking side by side . . . / I'm going to beat my woman, 'til I get satisfied' – Robert Johnson, from 'Me and the Devil Blues' (1937). The slave trade mingled African hedonism with New World Puritanism, inducing a moral ambivalence that survives into modern Cool.

powerful blues to the infusion of Puritan guilt into the slave psyche: 'This side of the blues did not come from Africa, but from the Puritan revival of the Great Awakening, the revival that spread across the American colonies more than two hundred years ago. It was an explosion of dread and piety that Southern whites passed onto their slaves and that blacks ultimately fashioned into their own religion.'[14] That seems a plausible enough explanation of how Johnson could sing with such conviction:

> Me and the devil was walking side by side
> Oooo, me and the devil was walking side by side
> I'm going to beat my woman, 'til I get satisfied.

This moral ambivalence passed straight from the blues, through rock 'n' roll and into successive popular musical forms like soul and hip-hop which have been among the prime carriers of Cool around the world.

Earlier we suggested that Cool can act as a defence mechanism against oppression and depression, but this defence does not come free of charge and this moral ambivalence is its price: a suburban middle-class teenager may have nothing materially in common with a slave in a levee camp, but psychologically they share the sexually confused, passive-aggressive tone of the blues.

But that is only one side of the coin. As Richard Wright goes on to say: '. . . the most astonishing aspect of the blues is that, although replete with a sense of defeat and down-heartedness, they are not intrinsically pessimistic; their burden of woe and melancholy is dialec-tically redeemed through sheer force of sensuality, into an almost exultant affirmation of life, of love, of sex, of movement, of hope'.[15] This aspect too has passed down into modern Cool – a creative, exuber-ant, Dionysian sensibility wholly at odds with all forms of puritanism (whether Christian, Islamic or communist). Any one of thousands of up-tempo 'Saturday night' blues would serve as an example here, but B.B. King's *Sweet Little Angel* captures the spirit perfectly:

> Asked my baby for a nickel, and she gave me a twenty-dollar
> bill (*twice*)
> Asked her for a little drink of liquor, and she bought me a
> whisky still

A direct line leads from there to Ian Dury's 'Sex and Drugs and Rock and Roll', one of the frankest manifestos that Cool has ever uttered.

Into the Cool

Throughout the first four decades of the twentieth century, jazz musicians were among the leading innovators and incubators of Cool attitude. Even during the 'Roaring '20s and the '30s, when as popular entertainers jazz men had to present a 'hot' face to their largely white audiences, off stage they were cultivating Cool. For example, Louis Armstrong may have acted the lovable clown while entertaining the white folks, but in reality he was a complex man, with an appetite for drink, dope and women, as well as being a virtuoso musician who revolutionized trumpet playing. (Anyone who doubts this should check out the story of how the line 'Richard Milhous Nixon I love you' came to be in Armstrong's hit song *Wonderful World*: after meeting Nixon, who was a fan of his, on an airliner Armstrong conned him into carrying his stash of marijuana through US Customs for him, hidden in his trumpet case.)

During the latter part of the '40s a more uncompromising generation of jazz musicians emerged, their great technical virtuosity honed by years of arduous touring in swing bands like Jay McShann's or Count Basie's. They felt a deep distaste for the white demand for easy dance music, and began to experiment with the hermetic style called bebop which was too fast for whites to dance to, and instead designed to showcase their dexterity and command of harmony and melody. Alto saxophonist Charlie Parker, perhaps the most accomplished of the boppers, explicitly compared his music with that of the European modernist composers Bartok and Stravinsky, and saw no reason why it should be taken less seriously. Some of the century's greatest musicians and composers, including Lester Young, Parker, Miles Davis and Charles Mingus practised their art, often for scant financial reward, under the rubric of this 'modern jazz'.

Modern jazz had aspirations beyond entertainment: it required a deep, subjective rapport to 'dig' this music, that is, to grasp it intuitively without reason or analysis. Most of the musicians led dissipated lives,

Some of this century's greatest musicians and composers, including Charlie Parker and Miles Davis (shown here at the Three Deuces, New York, in 1947) practised their art for scant financial reward under the rubric of 'modern jazz'.

and heroin addiction was regarded almost as a professional qualification. Following the premature drug-induced death of Parker, Miles Davis headed off in the direction that became known as the 'cool school' by lowering the tempo of bebop, and playing heavily on wistful minor-key blues melodies. On Davis's 1949 album *Birth of the Cool*, he and the alto sax-player, Lee Konitz, played 'as if in sight of some new musical world . . . more interested in texture and structure than grandstand barnstorming soloing'.[16] His classic album *Kind of Blue* of a decade later is invariably the only jazz album to feature in the Best Album of All Time polls. The cool style was picked up and refined by West Coast musicians, notably baritone saxophonist Gerry Mulligan and trumpeter-singer Chet Baker, and by the mid '50s a new (and comparatively lucrative) outlet for hard-pressed jazz musicians emerged to replace the smoky basement jazz club – the college concert. Where previously jazz had been treated with disdain by institutions of higher learning, now, as jazz critic James Lincoln Collier records, 'a jazz concert was a serious business – educational, uplifting. And in the middle of the '50s there came a surge in them that really amounted to a fad . . . '[17] But it was a fad mainly among the young educated whites. As another jazz critic has argued, 'Although some blacks were involved, at least briefly, with this "cool" movement, it was overwhelmingly a white phenomenon, both in its protagonists and its audience . . . In black neighbourhoods, cool jazz went virtually unnoticed.'[18]

A new synthesis called Third Stream emerged which incorporated techniques and instruments associated with the classical orchestra and was played by musicians with classical training like Dave Brubeck who had studied under Darius Milhaud. Brubeck and saxophonist Paul Desmond's contrapuntal playing on *Take Five* is probably the most famous (and best-selling) example of 'modern jazz' ever recorded, and it became the signature tune for the safe tendency in Cool. The Modern Jazz Quartet was lead by the scholarly-looking pianist John Lewis who held a masters degree from the Manhattan School of Music and played a buttoned-down kind of chamber jazz.

This was to be the last time that jazz was widely popular to a young white audience. Rock 'n' roll – which was in essence a modified version of the big band blues of the '40s fused with elements from country music – was soon to sweep away all other contenders for the throne of popular music. Black entertainers such as Little Richard, Chuck Berry, Jackie Wilson and Larry Williams were highly influential in the formative years of rock 'n' roll between 1955 and 1958, but it was a white working-class boy, Elvis Presley, who changed the rules forever. Sam Philips, the owner of Sun Records in Memphis had set out to find a pretty white boy who could sing as if he were black, but he could not have imagined how potent that combination would prove to be. Not only did Presley entice large numbers of white youth to listen to what they had previously considered 'race music' for the first time, but he reshaped the future of popular music: from now on image and attitude were going to be more important than musical virtuosity.

The history of rock 'n' roll has been rewritten so many times and it is not our intention to rehash it again. Suffice to say that what modern jazz had meant to a small band of striving black artists and their equally small Hip audience, rock 'n' roll opened up to a mass teenage audience in the late '50s; the music became a defining force in their lives, and set them apart for ever from their parents' generation. This was the moment in which Cool in its modern form broke out of the ghetto and into the mainstream of society, the true arrival of what we will later call the People's Modernism. One of the few thoughtful writers about rock music, Greil Marcus, saw that

> The best popular artists create immediate links between
> people who might have nothing in common but a response
> to their work, but the best popular artists never stop trying to

Elvis Presley (shown here *c*. 1947) reshaped the future of popular music; from now on, image and attitude would be more important than musical virtuosity. His manager, Colonel Tom Parker (left), parlayed that image into convertible currency.

understand the impact of their work on their audiences . . . The tension between community and self-reliance; between distance from one's audience and affection for it; between the shared experience of popular culture and the special talents of the artists who both draw on that shared experience and change it – these things are what make rock 'n' roll at its best a democratic art, at least in the American meaning of the word democracy.[19]

Elvis Presley was perhaps the first performer to understand the awesome power that Cool could exert over a mass audience, and even in his grotesque final incarnations as the obese, perspiring, jump-suited clown of the Las Vegas years, some remnants of this power still attached to him. Greil Marcus grasped this point too:

> . . . a self-made man is rather boring, but a self-made king is something else. Dressed in blue, red, white, ultimately gold, with a Superman cape and covered with jewels that no one can be sure are fake, Elvis might epitomize the worst of our culture – he is bragging, selfish, narcissistic, condescending, materialistic to the point of insanity. But there is no need to take that seriously, no need to take anything seriously. 'Aw, shucks,' says the country boy; it is all a joke to him; his distance is in his humor, and he can exit from this America unmarked, unimpressed, and uninteresting.[20]

CHAPTER THREE

A Whiter Shade of Cool

It seems to us indisputable that the roots of modern Cool lie in African (and later African-American) culture, but that should not blind us to the fact that phenomena very similar to our notion of Cool have arisen independently in other places and at other times. The modern version of Cool, as transmitted via popular music, films and television, will inevitably interact with, absorb, and be modified by these local attitudes in a very complex fashion, and it would take a far more comprehensive study than this to collect and catalogue all these variants, although we do have some tantalizing hints. It is obvious, for example, that the persecution of homosexuals in all societies, and for many centuries, led to the creation of subterranean styles and attitudes such as camp irony that not only closely resemble Cool but have had a considerable input into its modern forms, as we shall see in a later chapter.

Taking another example, who can doubt that there is a degree of overlap between our notion of Cool and the 'machismo' of Hispanic cultures, with its emphasis on appearance, male sexual adventurism and flirtation with death, as symbolized in the person of the toreador?

There may even be equivalents to Cool to be found in the ethic of the Samurai caste in Japan, or the warrior and bandit castes of India and East Asia. And what about that 'Anatolian smile' of Turkey, which film director Elia Kazan has described his émigré carpet-dealer father deploying as a universal tool for ingratiating, defusing, concealing and deceiving?

Studying behavioural subtleties from the perspective of Cool is of course fraught with difficulty, especially when it comes to cultures of which we have neither the language nor any personal experience. About Europe, we are on firmer ground, and what we know suggests that attitudes similar to modern Cool have existed here for centuries. However, they have tended to be the preserve of the aristocracy, of those who did not need to work and could devote their lives to seeking pleasure and cultivating their personalities. Robert Farris Thompson acknowledges this connection: 'Language in Africa and Europe shares notions of self-control and imperturbability, expressed under a metaphysical rubric of coolness, viz. notions of sang-froid and coolheadedness.'[1]

The virtue of emotional continence or economy was well-appreciated, for example in Renaissance Italy, where an attitude or philosophy called '*sprezzatura*' was deployed and admired by the courtiers of Italian princes, as described and prescribed in Baldessare Castiglione's *Book of the Courtier* (1516), a contemporary manual of rhetoric and etiquette. *Sprezzatura* was an attitude of aristocratic disdain, the cultivation of an appearance of effortlessness in accomplishing difficult actions (by well-rehearsed concealment of the effort that really went into them). The Italian verb *sprezzare* means to scorn or despise, and the chief modern historian of the concept Richard Lanham suggests that: 'Sprezzatura retains the force of its parent verb. It involves disdain. It declares, brags about, successful enselfment, a permanent incorporation in, addition to, the self. It satisfies because it publicly declares an enlarged self . . . the self is enriched, amplified, and as sign of amplification comes the effortlessness, the sprezzatura.'[2] That description, with its

'I have found quite a universal rule: and that is to avoid affectation in every way possible as though it were some rough and dangerous reef. Practice in all things a certain sprezzatura, so as to conceal all art and make whatever is done or said appear to be without effort . . . Then the Count replied: "Do you not see that what you are calling nonchalance in messer Roberto is really affectation, because we clearly see him making every effort to show that he takes no thought of what he is about, which means taking too much thought?"' – from Singleton, trans., *Il Cortegiano* (*The Book of The Courtier*) (1959). Baldassare Castiglione (1478–1529) in a portrait by Raphael (1514–15).

emphasis on the projection of self, comes very close to Cool in our sense.

Castiglione's book appears to have influenced aristocrats across the continent during the next few centuries; perhaps it influenced the British aristocracy, or maybe they evolved that 'unflappability' for which they are renowned quite separately. Aristocratic Cool, or hauteur, in many respects resembles the humbler forms of Cool, particularly in its tendency to frank amorality and love of illicit pleasures behind closed doors.

In the eighteenth and nineteenth centuries, this British proto-Cool came to be the preserve of beaus, fops, dandies, flaneurs and poseurs, mashers and swells who combined narcissism, nonchalance, wit and hedonism.[3] Those bare-headed aristocrats ascending the scaffold during the French Revolution demonstrated the psychic effectiveness of Cool even in the face of death, while the dialogue put into the mouth of the fictional Scarlet Pimpernel by Baroness Orczy was drolly Cool.

The First World War and Its Aftermath

Despite such teasing historical precedents, Cool, in the full sense with which we invest it, is an emotional style that belongs to the modern age, and it took the collapse of faith in organized religion and the trauma of two world wars to turn it into a mass phenomenon. For the white populations of America and Europe the unimaginable horrors of the First World War marked a watershed in the development of the Western psyche that prepared it for the coming of Cool. On the occasion of the 80th anniversary of the end of the First World War in 1998, a British commentator wrote that 'the degree of trauma associated with the 1914–18 War marked a departure not merely for the creation of new social forces but for the twentieth-century mind. The key elements of the modern mind – sceptical, individualistic, secular, non-deferential, living for the present – appear after the Great War.'[4] It is a commonplace of cultural criticism that the Great War, by destroying the remnants of nineteenth-century traditions of deference and self-denial inspired the various Modernist movements in the arts and social sciences that dominated intellectual life for the first two-thirds of this century. Although Modernism was largely consumed by the upper and middle classes (neither universal education nor suffrage had yet been won), it nevertheless sowed ironic seeds throughout the whole society that would only blossom after the Second World War, to contribute to Cool as we now know it. Paul Fussell summarized the depth and nature of this break beautifully by analysing the literature and diaries that came out of the war: 'Out of the world of summer, 1914, marched a unique generation. It believed in Progress and Art and in no way doubted the benignity even of technology. The word *machine* was not yet invariably coupled with the word *gun*.'[5] Fussell's use of irony in that last sentence acts out his thesis that the First World War was so much more horrible than anyone could have expected that people could bear to recall it only through irony, for example by juxtaposing the blue sky at the start of an attack with the red mud afterwards. Such irony was to become the only viable relation to the world for modern thinkers.

Modernism in culture was initially confined to small groups of avant-gardes, from the hedonistic flappers of the 'Roaring '20s' to those austere educated classes who developed what Stearns calls 'a new emotional culture' of rational child rearing and enlightened sexuality: planned parenthood, birth control and a tendency towards smaller families.[6] Among the working and lower-middle classes, Victorian morality, sexual abstinence and the regimentation of working life persisted until the '50s, when what we will later term 'The People's Modernism' finally arrived.

Nevertheless, some of the key themes of modern Cool were forged by avant-garde artists who achieved prominence in the aftermath of the First World War, most notably the Dadaists and the left-wing milieu of the Weimar republic which survived from 1919 to 1933. The programme of such groups was often self-consciously revolutionary, a determination to scandalize the bourgeoisie by mocking their culture, sexuality and political moderation. Under the looming shadow of Hitler and his Nazis, the nightclubs of Berlin rang to the seductive music of Kurt Weill and Lotte Lenya, while galleries and magazines displayed the vituperative caricatures of Georg Grosz and Otto Dix and in the theatres were to be heard the politically subversive poems and plays of Bertholt Brecht and Frank Wedekind.

Brecht, as both a committed communist and a philandering cynic (whose several different passports testified to his suspicion of all governments) could stand as the archetype of this inter-war Cool. Key Dada figures like Arthur Cravan, Man Ray or Marcel Duchamp might well

'I will not allow bitterness to quench my cigar's glow': Bertholt Brecht in 1927, around the time he composed *The Threepenny Opera*. Brecht's allegiance to Communism did not preclude his believing that anyone who did not ultimately pursue their own pleasure is a fool.

provide equally rich material, but Brecht has the advantage of opening his mind to us through his poetry. He expressed his detachment in sexual affairs with disarming directness in the lines:

> Forenoons in my rocking chair I sit
> Between a couple of women, days on end
> And I gaze upon them carelessly and say:
> Here you have a man on whom you can't depend.[7]

Brecht projected this Cool attitude to life onto his most famous character Macheath (aka Mackie Messer, aka Mack the Knife) in *The Threepenny Opera*, a work whose sole purpose is the excoriation of bourgeois sentimentality. Mackie, the nonchalant smooth-talking gangster, expert with the switchblade, personifies the bitter-sweet strain of Cool, a creature of the night who asks his lover 'Have you seen the Moon over Soho?' Puritanism and sentimentality are both anathema to the Cool character, and Brecht's allegiance to communism could not disguise the fact that in his opinion anyone who does not ultimately pursue their own pleasure is a fool ('I will not allow bitterness to quench my cigar's glow'). Brecht loathed sentimentality above all things and loved irony, was deeply cynical about sex and money ('Erst kommt das Fressen, dann kommt die Moral' [first comes food, then morality]) and loved to flirt with criminality, yet throughout his life he remained steadfast in his adherence to the one great principle of hope that had survived the horror of the Great War – that of the ultimate triumph of human goodness through socialism (with a Soviet face). He was even capable of writing po-faced eulogies to Stalin, although he could ironize these too:

> On my wall hangs a Japanese Carving
> The mask of an evil demon, decorated with gold lacquer
> Sympathetically I observe
> The swollen veins of the forehead, indicating
> What a strain it is to be evil.[8]

Within the personality of Brecht we can see contending those forces that for 40 years deterred Cool from emerging into the mass of society – it took the Holocaust, Hiroshima and the Cold War to destroy those final threads of faith. Perhaps the greatest irony is that Brecht's own attachment to communism was in the end sentimental (which may have been its only redeeming feature):

> The house painter speaks of great times to come.
> The woods still grow.
> The fields still bear.
> The cities still stand.
> Men still breathe. [9]

However, during these turbulent inter-war years Cool was a privilege reserved for bohemian milieus like Brecht's. Against the backdrop of the Great Depression, the collapse of currencies and the rise of dictatorships, life was a serious business for most people, for whom survival was a higher priority. While some of the middle classes (particularly those whom the Communist Party used to call 'progressives') adopted certain aspects of Modernism, they remained essentially conservative in their tastes – for them 'culture' still meant the traditional forms (the play, the novel, the poem) and great institutions (libraries, universities, theatres, museums, art galleries and symphony orchestras) which at that time were mostly financed by rich philanthropists. This was an élite culture, but one supported not only by the rich but also by the left-leaning 'working intelligentsia' which spanned professionals like doctors, lawyers, bankers, engineers, academics and those working-class 'organic intellectuals' (to borrow Gramsci's term) for whom self-improvement was an end in itself, rather than a means to professional advancement. It was not unusual for a keen trade-unionist to keep a piano in the parlour and have a child attending piano lessons (classical, not jazz). For the majority of young people during the inter-war years, amusements remained fairly innocent (drinking, dancing and furtive sex) and few rebellious working-class youth subcultures emerged until the '50s.

Cool irony and hedonism remained the province of cabaret artistes, ostentatious gangsters and rich socialites, those decadents depicted in Isherwood's *Goodbye to Berlin*, Scott Fitzgerald's *The Great Gatsby* and Waugh's *Brideshead Revisited*. Appropriately enough these same socialites loved to 'slum it' in those mean streets down which Philip Marlowe and Sam Spade, the grittily honest private eyes of hard-boiled crime fiction, must go in their weary pursuit of truth and justice, and in so doing trace the outlines of a new, whiter shade of Cool.

Peter Stearns suggests that in effect the seeds of a Cool outlook had been sown among this inter-war generation, but that germination was delayed, so that Cool became a widespread term for an appropriate emotional style only in the '60s, for the full measure of the culture occurred thirty or forty years after its effective inception.[10] In short, what deferred the emergence of Cool between the wars was a single remaining strand of faith, not in religion but in ideology (socialism and its evil twin fascism).

Postwar Cool

Angus Calder, echoing the common parlance in Britain post-May 1940, has dubbed the Second World War the 'People's War' because it was in several respects more 'democratic' than the First: the class divide between officers and men was less unbridgeable; through air warfare civilians were forced to share the suffering of the soldiers; for US troops at least, it brought black and white together in ways they would seldom experience in peacetime; and most importantly for our thesis, it brought the populations of Britain, Germany and France into intimate contact with Americans and American popular culture. From the late '40s onwards this American popular culture and affluence grabbed the imaginations of young people all over the world, to the great dismay of the paternalistic élites that still ruled official culture. The French intelligentsia of both left and right were outraged, while the British educated classes displayed a haughty indifference that smacked of an older aristocratic Cool. The war had brought to stricken Europe hundreds of thousands of GIs whose relaxed easy going manner must have been seen by young people of the time as the very embodiment of liberation; and with them came Lucky Strikes, nylons, music (not yet rock 'n' roll but rather swing and R&B) and Cool.

American Cool proved in the end to be more exportable than Soviet communism, which had appealed briefly to the Western working intelligentsia during the inter-war years. Those communist parties in France and Italy that remained loyal to the Soviet model after the war found they were facing a sceptical generation, and their influence rapidly faded.

The war had destroyed or disrupted the lives of millions and demobilization for the vast majority of the survivors meant a welcome return to the conventionality and tranquillity of domestic life. In the UK these ex-servicemen and women were the people who elected Clement Attlee's 1945 Labour Government and built the Welfare State, with the promise of security against a repeat of such calamities. For some of their children however, the experience of war had poisoned the very idea of domesticity, respectability and convention, and they concluded that 'society' itself was to blame and hence to be shunned. The emotional fall-out from the dropping of the Atom bomb, the psychological numbness that ensued from revelations of the Holocaust, the anxieties aroused by the escalating Cold War, all reinforced a sensibility among some young people – although still a tiny minority – which made them recoil from the respectability and stability that the mainstream craved. They opted out of Cold War politics, which they perceived as polarized between McCarthyism and Stalinism. For such people, both east and west of the 'Iron Curtain', Cool became a search for salvation in moments of individual epiphany rather than through collectively defined goals and ideals.

In those countries that had been occupied during the war and had produced resistance movements (particularly France and Italy) some of these young dissidents, most notably the group of intellectuals around Jean-Paul Sartre in Paris, grappled with the intractable problem of trying to reconcile individualism and Stalinism, using existentialism as the glue. Many more drifted toward anarchism or apolitical hedonism. The café, the corner coffee shop, the radical bookstore, the jazz club, the YMCAs, replaced the symphony hall as the site of culture, and the party cell as the site of political discussion. In 'the wakeful enthusiasm of the café' or in 'the ebullience, ecstasy and despair of the tavern',[11] to be Cool or Hip meant hanging out, pursuing sexual liaisons, displaying the appropriate attitude of narcissistic self-absorption, and expressing a desire to escape the mental straitjacket of all ideological causes.

Parents of all political persuasions were appalled by this disdainful new attitude that their children were displaying – Cool casually dismissed the post-war idealism that had built the United Nations and the Welfare State and which the older generation regarded as a decent recompense for war-time sacrifices. Cool was not especially sympathetic toward social activism, except perhaps in the one realm of anti-racism (or Civil Rights as it would then have been called). Take for example Louis Ginsberg, father of the poet Allen Ginsberg who later became a figure-head for both the beat movement and the '60s counter-culture: Louis, who was also a poet and an active New Deal socialist, wrote to his son while the latter was still at college, criticizing his decadent lifestyle and finally asking 'Where is your former, fine zeal, for a liberal, progressive, democratic society?'[12] Or take Polish-American novelist Jerzy Kosinski's father, a member of the Polish United Workers Party with roots in the old Lodz of élite culture and the working intelligentsia,

Marlon Brando defined the epoch when, in answer to the question 'What are you rebelling against Johnny?', he quipped: 'What have you got?' Laslo Benedek's 1953 film *The Wild One*.

who saw no virtue in this new subculture, telling his son 'Nothing clever was ever said in a café'.[13]

Cool rejected all kinds of overt sentimentality, which included publicly agonizing over the lot of the poor. Indeed the antagonism between street-Cool and social activism became a cliché of certain movies and novels of the time – from *On the Waterfront* (1954) and *The Blackboard Jungle* (1955) all the way to *West Side Story* (1957) – where the

James Dean's untimely death in a car crash in 1955 sealed his status as Cool's first martyr and saint.

stereotypical big-hearted teacher/cop/priest/social worker tries to inculcate social responsibility into street-wise Cool kids, whose response may be paraphrased as 'only suckers care'. That the activists were usually portrayed as winning the argument perhaps reflected the compulsory optimism of the mostly left-leaning screen-writers and directors rather than the reality.

So in the teeth of disapproval from both 'straight' society and the old left, Cool united a generation of disaffected artists, writers and intellectuals scattered across the globe who came of age in the '50s: in New York's Greenwich Village, on the Left Bank in Paris, in San Francisco's City Lights Bookstore, in the drinking clubs of London's Soho.

Support for the old high culture and a prejudice against this Cool subculture died hard among leftists, surviving even among those Frankfurt School Marxists who became gurus to the New Left in the '60s. For example Theodore Adorno in a letter to Herbert Marcuse, bemoaned 'the substitution of Beethoven's 9th with Jazz and Beat . . . the scum of the culture industry'.[14] While disgruntled ex-GIs were forming the first outlaw motorcycle gangs, and the beat poets were declaiming their strident verses, another Frankfurter, Max Horkheimer, indicted Cool directly for the anti-social behaviour of juvenile delinquents who have a cool, detached outlook on the world.

The new attitude found a special resonance behind the Iron Curtain where it offered relief from the earnestness of socialist propaganda and socialist realism in art. In the grim Polish industrial city of Lodz (often referred to as the Polish Manchester and comparable to Detroit), jazz 'the forbidden music' served Polish youth of the '50s much as it had served its black-American creators, both as personal diversion and a subterranean resistance to what they saw as a stultifying official culture. Some clubs featured live jazz performances, and their smoky, sexually charged atmosphere carried 'a message for which the puritanical values and monumental art of Marxist officialdom were an ideal foil'.[15] Tellingly, the word for 'cool' meaning low temperature in Polish, is 'chlodny' which has no subcultural association, and Polish youth use the English word 'cool'. Arriving in Poland via France, America and England, Polish Cool stimulated the film talents of a generation of artists, including Andrzej Wajda, Roman Polanski and other graduates of the Lodz Film School, as well as the novelist Jerzy Kosinski in whose clinical prose Cool tends towards the sadistic. In Prague, appropriately enough the

In flight from the earnestness of socialist realism, a generation of film makers of the Lodz school forged a uniquely Polish Cool. Zbigniev Cybulski in Andrzej Wajda's 1957 film *Ashes and Diamonds*.

capital of Bohemia, Cool flourished in the faded Art Deco splendour of the Cafe Slavia where a budding playwright Vaclav Havel used to hang out. Significantly, following the crushing of the Prague Spring by Soviet tanks in 1968, part of the dissident underground called itself the 'Jazz Section'.

The Beats

In Europe and America during the '50s Cool was becoming the province of white bohemians (even Bohemians) who increasingly sought to imitate the style of dissident 'Negro' subcultures. In America these ideas coalesced into a largely literary phenomenon now known as the beat movement or generation, whose founding figures included Jack Kerouac, Allen Ginsberg and William Burroughs: the name was intended to suggest their weariness and wariness under the oppression of respectable

To the beats, living fast and dying young seemed like a more radical challenge to the established order than any of the available political movements. William Burroughs (shown here c. 1966–7) nevertheless lived to a ripe old age, perhaps embalmed like one of his own characters by narcotics.

society. Norman Mailer's pivotal essay *The White Negro* (1957) explained to what extent these '50s hipsters were in thrall to Hip black values: 'If marijuana was the wedding ring, the child was the language of Hip . . . And in this wedding of the white and the black it was the Negro who brought the cultural dowry.'[16] In short, living fast and dying young seemed like a more radical challenge to the established order than any of the available political movements could offer. The beats regarded jobs, families, security, indeed any form of deferred gratification as dull and conformist. They opted out of work and civic duties to pursue immediate pleasures, claiming to be chasing a higher truth through oriental philosophies and experimentation with mind-expanding drugs.

Kerouac, for instance, claimed to have found an ancient mirror of his Cool – or Hip as they would more often call it at the time – values in Zen Buddhism ('I don't want to be a drunken hero of the generation suffering everywhere with everyone. I want to be a quiet saint living in a shack in solitary meditation of universal mind'[17]), while the poet Gary Snyder, who had studied Asian languages at Berkeley, went so far as to live in a Zen monastery in Japan. Other beats discovered an affinity with the Taoist texts of the *Tao Te Ching* and *I Ching*, while Allen Ginsberg adopted the Hindu holy rites of Hare Krishna. (This fascination with oriental religions was destined to be passed along by them to the '60s counter-culture.) Whether the detachment from worldly concerns advocated by Zen and Hindu masters really is of a kind with the ironic detachment of Cool writers in mid-twentieth-century America is questionable, and would provide meat for a whole study in itself. What is more certain is that those masters would not have approved of the debauched lifestyles that the beats led, particularly in the matter of drug and alcohol consumption. Kerouac once said, 'I've had my highest visions of Buddhist Emptiness when drunk'[18] and died a raging alcoholic. Most of the high profile exponents of post-war Cool, from the beats to Jackson Pollock, Miles Davis and Robert Mitchum, pursued hard, chaotic lives that revolved (sometimes literally) around drugs, booze, voracious sexuality and flirtations with criminality: quiet saints indeed.

This beat generation made its presence felt largely through ink on paper, in works such as Albert Camus' *The Outsider* and Kerouac's *On the Road*. For some of these writers Cool was a passive, introverted state concerned with protecting their fragile egos against a cruel world, but for Mailer it was more confrontational, going beyond mere non-conformist gestures to become a complete solution: 'The only life-giving answer to the deathly drag of American civilization is to tear oneself from the security of physical and spiritual certainty, to divorce oneself from society, to exist without roots, to set out on that uncharted journey with the rebellious imperatives of the self.'[19] Cool was beginning to be seen, in

Thom Gunn's words, as a 'posture for combat': in the grey corner The Man in the Grey Flannel Suit, in the blue corner the hipster. This intellectual ferment remained the province of self-proclaimed intellectuals often existing on the fringes of the criminal world. The poet Gregory Corso is a typical example: following a tragic childhood he spent time in a New York penitentiary for robbery, the perfect apprenticeship for a Hip literary career in '50s America, when Greenwich Village aspired to rival the Rive Gauche and needed its own robber-poet to pit against Jean Genet (in the same way that Jackson Pollock would go gunning for Picasso . . .).

A Sea Change

Increasingly discontented with the blandness of post-war life, and feeling an intense rivalry for the existentialist critiques that were emerging from Europe, a generation of liberal American social commentators began to criticize the alienating effects of the modern corporate capitalism that was being forged on the back of the post-war boom: to be *Growing Up Absurd* (Goodman 1954) in *The Affluent Society* (Galbraith 1952) was to be caught up in *The Pursuit of Loneliness* (Slater 1967); *The Organisation Man* (Whyte 1956) lost in *The Lonely Crowd* (Riesman 1952). They named their new enemies as *The Waste Makers* (1960) and *The Pyramid Climbers* (1962), all manipulated by *The Hidden Persuaders* (Packard 1957). These critiques were best-sellers, read by ordinary Americans, not only radical intellectuals. It was suddenly OK to feel a little daring, to be an individualist, to read *Playboy*, to buy a pair of Italian shoes, even perhaps to wear shades to the office . . .

Post-war Cool was at least in part an expression of war-weariness, and it vehemently rejected the 'hot' nationalistic ideals that the Cold War and McCarthyism were stirring up in favour of a detached and cool-under-fire attitude that cared for neither president nor country.

The archetypical GIs depicted in Sam Fuller's *The Steel Helmet* (1951) or Norman Mailer's first novel *The Naked and the Dead*, with their helmets casually unstrapped and what may be their last cigarettes dangling from their lips, were not the mindlessly patriotic fighting machines of war propaganda, but resigned, deeply democratic, even thoughtful individuals. For Hollywood an older American role model, the rugged frontier individualist and gung-ho patriot typified by John Wayne, was passing away as a tenable image, forced out by the new Cool pose with its own generation of heroes: Brando, Dean, Newman, Clift. Hollywood saw the potential of Cool, and by so doing reinforced its potency in the popular imagination. Just three roles, in *East of Eden*, *Rebel Without a Cause* and *Giant* were enough to establish James Dean as a Cool original, and his untimely death in a car crash sealed his status as Cool's first martyr. To thousands of young people he was a rebel *with* a cause, and that cause was escape from the suffocating web of family ties, school, suburban respectability and labour discipline that the new 'mass society' imposed. Marlon Brando defined the epoch in his role as the leather-clad leader of a motorcycle gang in *The Wild One*, when in answer to the question 'What are you rebelling against Johnny?' Brando quips laconically 'What have you got?' The age of the anti-hero had dawned and white folks too, were learning how to be Cool.

CHAPTER FOUR

That's Cool Too . . .

The outsider pose that the beats had refined appealed to a new generation of radical dissenters who were congregating by the early '60s around the issues of free speech, Civil Rights, opposition to nuclear weapons and the Vietnam War. Although politics may have provided its initial impetus, this rebellion soon broadened into an attack on bourgeois lifestyles in general, offering as an alternative a hedonistic 'counter-culture' based on sex and drugs and rock 'n' roll. The sartorial style this '60s counter-culture adopted was so different from that of the '50s hipster that with hindsight it is difficult to believe the phenomena were related, but beneath surface appearances there was a great deal of continuity. For example it was no coincidence that adherents of the counter-culture came to be called 'hippies': in the '50s Hip had been a synonym for Cool, signifying knowingness, or a shared knowledge of secrets denied to squares. This meaning carried over directly into the counter-culture, captured perfectly in Bob Dylan's line 'Something is happening here, but you don't know what it is, do you, Mr Jones?' (*Ballad of a Thin Man*, 1965). The word 'cool' itself passed into hippy usage, although during the '60s it acquired a subtly altered connotation of soundness or safety: one end of a spectrum whose further extreme was 'wild'. 'He's cool' or 'everything's cool' would often be said to defuse some fraught situation (usually involving drugs). There was even continuity between the people and places of the beat generation and the new counter-culture, as many beat poets including Corso, Ferlinghetti, Snyder and Ginsberg were recognized and revered as precursors and pioneers of the new movement, and became popular figureheads (witness Ginsberg's presence at the 1966 San Francisco Human Be-In). Most of the early counter-culture manifestations occurred in the Bay area around San Francisco and Berkeley, the very same terrain that had nurtured the beats. And like the beats, hippies were drawn to black culture – particularly the music, although now it was R&B and soul rather than jazz.

The flamboyant hippy style could hardly have looked more different from the button-down shirts and shades of the Hip '50s jazz musician. Where many hipsters had parodied the garb of the straight businessman, by wearing sharper suits, thinner ties and more pointed shoes, hippies abandoned twentieth-century Western costume altogether in favour of brightly coloured ethnic styles – Mexican, Indian (both American and Asian), Moroccan, Afghan – and historical references to Romanticism or medieval and Tudor dress modes. The emblematic style, the wearing of long hair (with moustaches and beards for men), was an unambiguous rejection of the cropped, clean-shaven look that has been the emblem of puritanism throughout history. Ragged denim replaced the hipster's suit; long hair replaced the crew cut; very loud rock replaced the muted tones of Cool jazz; and marijuana, hashish and LSD replaced heroin as the Hip drugs. This radical changing of appearance, as each successive generation sought to differentiate itself from its parent's or elder sibling's clothing styles and slang, continues to the present day, but beneath such changes of image persists that blend of hedonism and narcissism that makes up Cool.

It is tempting to view the '60s counterculture as manifesting Warm and Wet rather than Cool tendencies. The truth is more subtle.

For just a few years the counter-culture wrought a striking transformation on the nature of Cool, by grafting onto its rebellious individualism a broader desire for social change. For the '50s hipster, Cool expressed rejection of the perceived hypocrisies of 'square society' in a passive, nihilistic and introverted way. It wasn't Cool to expose social inequities, still less to do anything about reforming them – just look good, stay high and tend your own patch. The hippies didn't want to hide away in dark night-clubs, but preferred to parade publicly in all their finery at Woodstock and Monterey and to proselytize to all the youth of the world. Cool had, however briefly, switched from a passive to an active attitude. Anarchic, dopey and disorganized although it was the counter-culture, for a short while, aspired to mass influence, sought to right injustices and to change society in its own colourful and free-wheeling image. What precisely triggered this sizeable protest movement – whose novelty was that it was largely based on age, rather than class, gender, religion, nationality or ethnicity – still awaits a truly adequate analysis and explanation, but we can sketch a few of its preconditions. In both the USA and to a lesser degree in the UK, by the mid-60s young people had been granted an unprecedented degree of economic independence, thanks to the long post-war economic boom. Access to higher educational institutions (if not yet their governance) had been democratized and expanded. The mass media (in particular cinema, television and vinyl music records) now had the ability to spread ideas very quickly around the world. Last, and perhaps most crucially, the invention of the contraceptive pill freed young people from many of the biological obstacles to free sexual activity. Social regulations that had been developed to maintain order in industrial society suddenly appeared arbitrary, unnecessary and oppressive.

Heavy Scenes

The reasons for 'dropping out' and adopting the Cool stance were clearly not the same for white, mostly middle-class hippies as they had been for the young blacks and Latinos of the inner cities. For the latter, Cool was a defence mechanism that helped them to retain some personal integrity in a world which continually undervalued and disrespected them. For white counter-culture radicals Cool was a more confrontational posture, a statement that even though they were not excluded from capitalist affluence, they chose to reject it in favour of something more egalitarian and 'authentic'. (It would be only slightly too cruel to describe this as a form of attitudinal 'slumming'). The counter-culture embellished Cool with an extraordinarily diverse range of exotic beliefs – ranging all the way from bomb-throwing anarchism and revolutionary socialism, through Buddhism and Hindu mysticism, to the psychotic paganism of Charles Manson's 'Family' – and the only thread uniting all these imported ideologies was that they must be as offensive as possible to democratic, capitalist, Protestant, white, Anglo-Saxon values. Some political radicals who joined the counter-culture tried to import neo-Marxist critiques of capitalism of varying degrees of subtlety, but these were never espoused by more than a very small minority. At the opposite extreme were those who adopted elements of Hindu and Buddhist mysticism, and tended to explain everything as the working out of karma.

In between these extremes, the majority of participants in the counter-culture constructed for themselves a rather loosely-woven opposition to what they perceived as straight society's war-mongering, greed and sexual repression, perhaps best epitomized by John Lennon and Yoko Ono's 'bed protest'. There emerged a 'lowest common denominator' level of rejection of the established order on aesthetic, moral and psychological grounds that could be shared by just about anyone who – by dress and lifestyle – announced themselves to be part of the counter-culture, regardless of any more specific grievances they may hold.

This Hip consensus saw straight society as repressive in several senses: it repressed people's emotions by demanding sexual and emotional continence and enforcing 'respectable' behaviour in public and the workplace; it repressed freedom of personal expression, more specifically the freedom to wear what you liked, to live without working and to take drugs; and it repressed truth by censorship and the keeping of state secrets (often of a military nature, since the Vietnam War was in progress). To be Hip one had both to acknowledge this repression, and to oppose it by dressing and living in an approved manner: sympathetic middle-class liberals might pass the first test and thus be described as 'cool', but they failed the second.

This perception of being repressed by the dominant culture underpinned the counter-culture's whole belief system. Although there was outrage at specific instances of actual repression – racist violence, police brutality toward demonstrators, dope busts, newsreel footage of Vietnam atrocities – this feeling of oppression was shared by thousands of young people who had not personally experienced any of these things, but merely felt their aspirations for greater personal freedom were being smothered by an excessively puritanical moral order.

Commentators such as Daniel Bell (*The Coming of Post-Industrial Society* [1973], *The Cultural Contradictions of Capitalism* [1976] and Thomas Frank (*The Conquest of Cool* [1998]), have remarked that by the mid-60s the post-war economic boom and the changing composition of modern industry had created the potential – from a marketing viewpoint, the imperative – to extend the boundaries of personal freedom, especially in matters of consumption and sexual behaviour. However, the prevailing adult morality remained puritanical, frozen by the experience of fighting two world wars, the labour disciplines of pre-war heavy industry, and the new tensions of the Cold War (as so wittily depicted in Daniel Ross's 1999 movie *Pleasantville*).

Hence where the beats had cultivated an unworldly detachment from commercial concerns, the '60s counter-culture (its oriental gurus notwithstanding) steered Cool in an altogether more materialistic direction toward the marketplace. Those *Hidden Persuaders* of Madison Avenue were becoming Hip themselves – Hip to the fact that 'hip' was a way into the hearts and wallets of the kids who formed their key market for clothing, music and soft drinks. Thomas Frank documents the way advertisers discovered in the early '60s how the cliquey solidarity implicit in Cool made possible sophisticated new strategies for brand differentiation which still rule today: Coke versus Pepsi, Nike versus Reebok, Reebok versus Adidas, Adidas versus Fila ... The counter-culture, far from expressing a demand for proletarian revolution, was unwittingly ushering in a new phase of capitalism. Perhaps not so unwittingly, for despite occasionally giving vent to revolutionary rhetoric, few members of the counter-culture wanted to overthrow capitalism on the Bolshevik model: most merely wanted to replace the uptight war-generation mentality with a Cooler more hedonistic one.

The Cult of Authenticity

In addition to perceiving straight society as repressive, counter-culture radicals also believed it to be somehow 'inauthentic'. Straight people didn't express what they were feeling; politicians didn't tell the truth; manufacturers created 'plastic' (i.e. tacky) products with built-in obsolescence; advertisers created false needs; food was contaminated with pesticides and additives. Best-selling exposés such as Rachel Carson's *Silent Spring* (1962) and Vance Packard's *The Hidden Persuaders* and *The Waste Makers* were influential in forming these attitudes.

The counter-culture sought its own notions of purity and authenticity to counterpoise what it saw as corrupted values. Ever since the days of slavery Cool had expressed resistance to authority through creative and innovative hair-styles, clothes and music, but the counter-culture elevated this process from handicraft to artisanal or even industrial status: hippies literally tried to build a new world, or at least an alternative economy. Vegetarian, wholefood and macrobiotic cafés sprang up all over the USA (and to a lesser extent in Europe), alongside collectives distributing brown rice and other esoteric foodstuffs. Shops and stalls selling homespun clothes and jewellery appeared, while the UK saw (at a rather more expensive end of the market) an explosion of radical fashion design from Ossie Clarke, Mr Freedom and Biba.

An important sartorial trend – already evident in the '50s with Dean and Brando – was the wholesale adoption of blue denim, the traditional working garb of the American field worker (black and white) and the cowboy: that is, of a more 'authentic' pre-industrial economy. This phenomenon promoted the denim jean manufacturers Levi Strauss and Lee Cooper into powerful forces in the global clothing industry, as well as innovators in youth advertising (which is where this book started).

Hippy entrepreneurs promoted a new breed of psychedelic rock bands, often creating new music venues for them by renting dilapidated property in poor sections of cities. In music too authenticity was the goal, sought in black music and folk music as opposed to the schmaltzy Broadway show tunes of the parents' generation or the too-scrubbed white vocalists of the commercial pop charts. Blues and folk had already become popular among Civil Rights activists in the very early '60s, and electrified urban blues and soul came to occupy a similar place later in the decade. A generation of innovative new British rock bands – The Beatles, The Yardbirds, The Rolling Stones, The Kinks, The Who and many more – all cut their teeth playing straight copies of US blues, R&B, Tamla/Motown and soul, and even helped to re-export their interest back to white teenagers in the USA. Major blues artists like B.B. King – who had been topping the black R&B charts for decades but was largely unknown to white audiences – broke through to be accepted by the rock audience, playing at the Fillmore West and, in an ironic reversal, performing as opening act for The Rolling Stones. In San Francisco the ex-DJ Sly Stone put together the Family Stone, the definitive Hip band which featured black and white, male and female members and played a fusion of the electronic innovations of psychedelic rock with the rhythms and stabbing brass of black soul: the influence of the form they created can be traced into '70s funk and today's house music and hip-hop.

As an antidote to the 'lies' of the straight press, a rash of 'underground' magazines, newspapers and comics appeared, made possible by IBM's recent invention of the relatively cheap and portable golf-ball typesetter, by cheap web offset printing and the advertising dollars of the hippy rock entrepreneurs. These publications combined radical politics and opposition to the Vietnam War with deliberately and comically obscene material, such as the cartoons of Robert Crumb and S. Clay Wilson designed to shock the bourgeoisie as they had not been shocked since Dada. If any artistic genre stood for everything the counter-culture detested, it would have to be the sentimental 'family entertainment' cartoons of Walt Disney, and these underground cartoonists set out with enthusiasm to subvert the form for ever (some indeed wound up in court for making too free with images of Mickey Mouse, Snow White and Rupert the Bear).

Hippies also sought to transcend the inauthentic emotions of straight society – which they considered to be at the same time sentimental and 'uptight' (i.e. puritanical) – by espousing in their place an intense romanticism and eroticism. In *The Culture of Narcissism* (1979), Christopher Lasch described how this cult of emotional authenticity could be seen at work in psychiatry and child-rearing advice in the USA as early as the '50s, characterized by the injunction to 'get in touch with your feelings' and the perception that 'all feelings are legitimate'. The counter-culture was created by the children of such advice, and these ideas found a fertile soil in which to bloom. In short it became Cool to express emotions, although only intense and 'authentic' kinds of emotion. The terminology of transactional psychologist Eric Berne, whose *Games People Play* (1964) was a best-seller, infiltrated counter-culture vocabulary in phrases like 'head games', a derogatory term for insincere and overly-rational manipulative behaviour.

In fact the hippies reinvented many aspects of nineteenth-century romanticism, including a heightened role for the imagination; the exuberant outpourings of personal feeling; an anti-scientific irrationalism and fascination with the mysterious, exotic and supernatural; a heightened empathy with nature and an excessive veneration of creative individuals such as artists (and now rock stars). They sought to avoid unpleasant and negative emotions (often by liberal self-medication with marijuana and acid) and to replace them with 'good vibes' or positive feelings. Sexual jealously and possessiveness were discouraged as another aspect of straight society's repressive influence. In such hippy attitudes we can detect the roots of that 'touchy-feely' confessional tendency so prevalent in today's popular culture, which at first sight appears to represent the antithesis of Cool. Indeed it is sometimes tempting to view the counter-culture as a whole as manifesting Warm and Wet rather than Cool tendencies. But the truth is, we believe, more subtle: the counter-culture was Cool's (doomed) attempt to become what it is not, by proselytizing, converting and embracing rather than excluding and mocking.

Moreover this hippy romanticism was often as much an adopted stance as the aloof arrogance of '50s Cool (parodied by Henry Winkler's Fonz). It is the role-playing itself that constitutes Cool – part of what the sociologist David Matza in *Delinquency and Drift* (1964) described as a process of construction of a subterranean identity – and beneath both stances lay a similar sense of ironic detachment from the affairs and concerns of straight society. No-one who lived through those times could doubt that beneath the mock orientalism lay total detachment – you might vigorously contradict someone's opinion only to receive the blissed-out reply 'That's Cool too, man', a gambit that survives today in the ubiquitous 'Whatever . . .'

Hollywood Gets Hip

San Francisco may be indelibly associated with hippydom in the popular imagination, but in fact no place was more affected by this 'revolution' than Hollywood. It was not only that the counter-culture provided new content for the movies, but it changed forever the lifestyle of the producers, directors and actors who made them. The stranglehold of an older generation of moguls who had been imposing their middle-class taste on the movie business for decades was suddenly and dramatically broken by a generation of Hip young directors who opened the way to today's amoral, blockbuster-fixated Hollywood.

The hippies themselves proved a poor subject for movies, and most films with explicit counter-culture themes look embarrassingly dated today. However, a new influx of counter-culture-inspired directors created an artistic renaissance in the early '70s, steering away from the smug safe subjects of old Hollywood towards a new brutal realism, in movies like *The Graduate* (1967), *Bonnie and Clyde* (1967), *The Wild Bunch* (1969), *MASH* (1970) and *The Godfather* (1972). If Marlon Brando's character Johnny in *The Wild One* (1953) had stood for the '50s brand of Cool, then perhaps the most obviously iconic character of '60s Cool ought to be Dennis Hopper's Billy in *Easy Rider* (1967). However, McMurphy, the irrepressible anti-hero of Ken Kesey's *One Flew Over the Cuckoo's Nest* (1962), memorably portrayed on film by Jack Nicholson, makes a far more interesting figurehead, sitting as he does as a transitional figure between '50s and '60s modes of Cool.

Peter Biskind's gossipy and picaresque study of Hollywood, *Easy Riders, Raging Bulls* (1998), describes well this revolution and shows how the young Turks sent shockwaves through the industry:

> It is not only the violence of Bonnie and Clyde, not only their refusal to say they were sorry that antagonized 'them'; it was the flair and energy with which the film pits the hip and the cool against the old, straight and stuffy. It says 'fuck you' not only to a generation of Americans who were on the wrong side of the generation gap, the wrong side of the war in Vietnam, but also to a generation of Motion Picture Academy members that had hoped to go quietly, with dignity. *Bonnie and Clyde* made that impossible.[1]

The stereotypical Hollywood producers of the '40s and '50s had dressed like gangsters (and treated their writers and directors accordingly) and Biskind records the moment of their overthrow by hip managers such as John Calley: 'Under Calley, Warners became the class act in town. Urbane and witty, he gave the impression that he was somehow above it all . . . He was so Hip he didn't even have a desk in his office, just a big coffee table covered with snacks, carrot sticks,

Old Hollywood had flirted with the more aristocratic modes of Cool, but Warren
Beatty's 1967 film *Bonnie and Clyde* changed that at a stroke; it said 'up yours' to
a generation of Motion Picture Academy members who had hoped to retire with
dignity. Cary Grant and Grace Kelly in Hitchcock's 1955 film *To Catch a Thief*;
Warren Beatty on set in the '60s.

hard-boiled eggs and candy.'[2] Calley created an atmosphere congenial to the new generation of film makers:

> The production executives put in long hours, but they dressed in work-shirts and jeans instead of suits. Wells wore jeans. Sanford wore sandals, and fixed his long hair in a ponytail . . . Five o'clock in the afternoon, instead of the clinking of ice in a glass would be the aroma of marijuana . . . It was sort of an asset to be into pot and acid. We were all hippies.[3]

The young Turks set about reconnecting themselves with European and Japanese Cool aesthetics by avidly consuming the films of Kurosawa, Fellini, Truffaut and Rene Clair. It is probably no coincidence that Stanislavsky's Method conquered Hollywood around this time, so that the house-style for Hollywood actors (outside of 'arthouse' movies) became essentially to play oneself. This can be seen as an effect of Cool's concern for authenticity, truth and revelation which actually leads it to a distrust of acting itself, as somehow bogus and untrue to the self. A famous story relates how Laurence Olivier, encountering Dustin Hoffman off the set exhausting himself by running in order to depict exhaustion on screen said to him 'My dear boy, have you ever considered *acting*.' As an aside, the current vogue for fly-on-the-wall documentary on UK television may be as much to do with the arrival of a Cool generation of programme controllers whose attitudes were formed in the wake of the '60s counter-culture, as it is with the undoubted cheapness of the format. Witness also the extraordinary strictures against artifice imposed on themselves by filmmakers of Lars von Trier's neo-realist *Dogme 95* group.

Politics is Pig Shit

For most of its participants the '60s counter-culture was profoundly apolitical, or even anti-political: 'Politics is Pig Shit' was a popular slogan, 'pigs' being a derogatory term for the police and other authorities. Most hippies believed all politicians of both left and right to be liars, thieves and warmongers, and although they may have offered temporary allegiance to some left-wing causes – such as the anti-Vietnam War movement – for the most part they believed that salvation was a personal, not a political matter. For example the cult surrounding the image of Che Guevara in the late '60s might suggest a deep sympathy for socialist revolution on the Cuban model, but in truth it was the personality of Guevara as a romantic (and very handsome) rebel that was being venerated. The counter-culture leant toward extreme libertarianism, 'do your own thing' being the closest to a political manifesto it ever produced, and such libertarianism was an uneasy partner to any sort of socialism or social democracy. Ironically, in its demands for total freedom from policing, and for economic self-sufficiency, the counter-culture had more in common than most would now care to admit with old traditions of right-wing American frontier individualism – a strain of individualism that now survives mostly among the militias of Montana who despise hippy morality as the root of America's decline. Over the course of the next decade it was not too arduous an ideological journey for many former counter-culture adherents to embrace Reaganism and Thatcherism (in economics at least).

Many of the obsessions of counter-culture political activists revolved around exposing conspiracies, from the Kennedy Assassination to Watergate, a passion that has been inherited by today's Internet culture. For example the paranoid contention that the US Government is covering up visits by aliens in flying saucers first took root in the '60s. Kennedy's assassination in 1963 can be seen as a major turning point in the history of Cool. Prior to that calamity various forms of liberal social activism, the Peace Corps or Civil Rights marches, might have been considered Cool and Kennedy embodied (in his glamorous public image, and his then unknown private sexual adventurism) the idea that change was possible and that a younger generation was coming to power. That may have been a fantasy in real political terms, but it was a widespread and potent fantasy – Kennedy was the first Cool US president, and the last until Bill Clinton's ascension to office. Following Kennedy's violent death all these possibilities seemed closed off in an instant, to be replaced by paranoid, traumatized, anti-political attitudes. This paranoia affected thousands of young people who would be attracted to the counter-culture, and it introduced a new and permanent component into that psychological synthesis that we are calling Cool, making it the deadly enemy of any form of concealment or artifice, of every sort of taboo – everything must be revealed, everything must be seen, everything must be attempted.

There were small, although briefly influential, factions within the counter-culture that adhered to different forms of revolutionary social-ism, some inspired by the fragmented Trotskyist movement that emerged

Should you doubt that Kennedy was Cool, look at the haircut, the smile and the sexual escapades, not at his policies.

after the twentieth Soviet Congress and the Red Army's invasion of Hungary, while others took their inspiration from older anarcho-syndicalist traditions. However, as we remarked in the previous chapter, the official parties of the socialist left exhibited precisely the same stern puritanism that hippies associated with the ruling establishment, and often to an even higher degree. For one of the authors this fact was brought home on discovering that the Communist Party of Great Britain didn't share his taste for the electric urban blues of Muddy Waters and Buddy Guy which it rejected as 'tainted by the decadence of Tin Pan Alley' in favour of the politically-sound banjo twanging of Pete Seeger. Bob Dylan arrived at a similar conclusion when he abandoned protest songs for surreal electrified rock, and was called 'Judas' for his pains.

Indeed it is hard to escape the conclusion that, outside the ranks of a minority of hippy-radicals, the mainstream counter-culture actually rejected working-class culture and politics more vehemently than that of the middle classes. In the USA particularly, the liberal middle classes were less hostile to counter-cultural values than were the more religious and conservative working classes. Some sections of liberal middle-class opinion were quite supportive, leading to grotesque juxtapositions such as the interview with Fidel Castro that appeared in *Playboy* magazine among the soft-core porn and cocktail recipes. By and large hippies saw working-class manners as conservative, sentimental and sometimes downright threatening. For example, one of the formative films of that era, *Easy Rider*, had as its villains two rural working-class 'rednecks' who shoot dead the hippy heroes for no better reason than dislike of their appearance. This hostility was real enough off the screen, as anyone who hitch-hiked in the USA during the late '60s will testify. In the UK it is significant that the high period of counter-cultural revolt from 1967 to 1970 coincided with Labour rather than Conservative governments.

Nihilists, One More Effort . . .

A few libertarian political groups did reject the puritanism of the barely de-Stalinized socialist left. In the USA there were political groups, typified by the yippies, who submerged themselves in counter-culture hedonism staging jokey anti-war protests and smoking dope in public places. By their insistence on spelling Amerika with a 'k' in their literature they sought to convince themselves of a spurious moral equivalence between American imperialism and Nazism.

More serious, and in hindsight far more influential, were the intellectual French rebels of the Situationist International (SI), who had emerged from the post-Surrealist art world rather than via conventional left politics, and who were most famous for supplying the more pithy slogans used during the student revolt of May 1968. Their leading

The Situationists held that capitalism and socialism were converging into a new kind of totalitarian synthesis, whose principle of control was the manufacture of celebrity by the mass media. This SI cartoon strip was fly-posted in London in 1968.

Members of the Situationist International attempt to deflect the steamroller of history . . .

theorist Guy Debord set out the core Situationist ideas in his book *The Society of the Spectacle* (1967) in which (very crudely summarized) he held that capitalism and socialism were converging into a new kind of totalitarian synthesis whose principle of control was the manufacture of celebrity by the mass media, mesmerizing the populace into imitative consumption and removing almost all need for actual physical repression. Given this perspective it is not surprising that the SI despised the counter-culture – as it did the political left – because it correctly foresaw that counter-cultural revolt would be absorbed to become just another aspect of 'the Spectacle'. According to the SI's analysis, nihilistic teenage street gangs, or the looters during the Watts and Detroit 'race' riots of 1964–5, were more radical than any left-wing activist because they took what they wanted with no respect for bourgeois law. This admiration for the freedom implied by the criminal act, inherited from a long European anarchist tradition, was to be the lasting legacy of the Situationists after Debord disbanded the SI in 1972.

In point of fact the Situationists' embrace of criminality had been conditional, expressed in their formula, 'nihilists, one more effort if you would become revolutionaries', which insisted that those who had freed themselves from the bonds of bourgeois conventionality via crime must take a further step into consciously revolutionary action. However, like Nietzsche's hope that mankind could surpass itself to bring forth the Superman, or Marx's hope that the state would wither away, this last step proved to be insurmountable, and all that remained in the minds of many who were influenced by the SI's ideas was an erroneous belief that crime is already revolutionary. A bit of thieving is easier (and more fun) than reading *The Society of the Spectacle*, and by the '70s the next genera-tion of revolting youth, the punks, had embraced a subtly-corrupted sub-situationism with great enthusiasm. The criminal underworld has for centuries been a wellspring of Cool style, but this debased version of the Situationist thesis finally provided an intellectual dimension to the association – it became Cool to be criminal.

In Debord's short autobiographical essay *Panegyric*, published five years before his suicide, he offers a glimpse of his youthful fascination with the '50s French street gang culture of the '*blouson noir*':

> In the zone of perdition where my youth went as if to complete its education, one would have said that the portents of an imminent collapse of the whole edifice of civilization had made an appointment. Permanently ensconced there were people who could only be defined negatively, for the good reason that they had no job, followed no course of study, and practised no art. Many of them had participated in the recent wars, in several of the armies that had fought over the continent . . . The remainder, who were five or six years younger, had come there directly, because the idea of the family had begun to dissolve, like all others.[4]

This is an eloquent description of that post-war anomie that nour-ished the spread of Cool, and the passage hints intriguingly that the Situationists may have even owed a small debt to Cool, although one they repaid many times over by making nihilism intellectually respectable.

Cooling Britannia

So far we have proceeded as if the '60s counter-culture developed identically on both sides of the Atlantic, but this was not at all the case. There was a complex process of cross-fertilization, with trends in clothes and music in particular crossing and re-crossing the Atlantic. For example the mod subculture that swept through Britain in the early '60s – spawning bands like The Rolling Stones, The Who and The Kinks – was influential in the USA in reviving interest in their own black R&B artists. Similarly the work of UK fashion designers like Ossie Clarke and Mary Quant fed into the sartorial style of US counter-culture. Nevertheless, there were also quite significant differences between the way the counter-culture emerged and developed between the USA and the UK.

The parental culture that British hippies had to rebel against was both less affluent and less sexually confident than its American counterpart. While not ferociously puritanical, it was possessed by a curious voluntary asexuality that arose between the two wars among the British middle and working classes and is parodied by the title of the long-running farce, *No Sex Please, We're British* but dignified, ennobled even in David Lean's film *Brief Encounter*. The social historian Ross McKibbin has observed that in the early '50s half the married population of England claimed to have had no sexual partners prior to their spouse. Tempered in the shared sacrifices of the Second World War, Britain had a more collective and less aggressively individualist culture than that of the USA, possessing a streak of undemonstrative, deep-yet-slightly-grudging altruism that George Orwell famously described as 'decency'. In the '50s and '60s imported American Cool set about demolishing that decency.

But importing Cool into Britain also transformed it in significant ways, making it more ironic and more class conscious. An emerging British underground had to define itself in opposition to a safe,

respectable, collectivist popular culture prevalent in the '50s and '60s –
the world of the Royal Variety Show, the BBC Light Programme and
the Black and White Minstrel Show. Anything that smacked of working
class respectability became deeply Uncool, while wide-boys, spivs and
lovable (from a distance) East End gangsters like the Kray brothers
became venerated figures. As an interesting aside, McKibbin, in speaking
of a dance craze of the late '30s, the 'Lambeth Walk', comments that

> the Lambeth and coster walks were strikingly like those 'coon
> dances', the cakewalk and ballin' the jack, which were very
> popular in the music-halls of East and South London in the
> 1890s. Both were swaggering walks, dependent on a rolling
> motion of heel and foot . . . cultural relationships between the
> United States and England in the inter-war years appear not
> so one-sided but more complicated, with movements in both
> directions.[5]

These are just some of the indications that the working-class neighbourhoods of London, Glasgow and other UK cities may have indigenous
notions of Cool that go back way before the '60s.

This emerging counter-culture provided an escape route for many
working-class British kids who otherwise faced a life of tedium in the
car plant or on the milk-bottling line, as testified to by the biographies of
rock stars from The Beatles to The Clash. It would be hard to exaggerate
the feeling of liberation that discovering, appropriating and transforming American popular music gave to this post-war generation of young
Britons, impelling them to reject what they saw as the grey conformist
culture of their parents' generation. A distinctively British strain of
counter-cultural revolt emerged, whose distinguishing characteristics
included a deep respect for black-American music (at a time when
US record charts were still segregated) and a unique strain of ironic
and surrealistic gallows humour that drew from older British comic

traditions, but was honed to a particularly keen edge during the two Wars. The *Goon Show* begat *Monty Python* which begat *Not the Nine O'Clock News* which begat *Blackadder* which begat the *Fast Show*. This British fine-tuning of Cool has been exported back across the Atlantic, through the phenomenon the Americans called 'Beatlemania' and the popularity of *Monty Python* on US public TV, and it affected the development of American Cool for the better, pushing it in a more humorous and liberal direction.

CHAPTER FIVE

Cool Cracks Up

In the early '70s the counter-culture imploded in a welter of violence, hard drugs and bad vibes, but although it had failed to fill the world with peace and love, it had unknowingly propelled Cool into the mainstream of society. What had in the '50s been a minority attitude, cultivated in the semi-secrecy of dark night clubs had now been exposed to the daylight, and more importantly to the media spotlight. Cool may appear to have vanished between the '70s and the '90s, but in fact it was there in the bloodstream of every new youth fashion designer and every advertising creative director, mutating into dozens of different forms, from heavy metal to punk to hip-hop. At first the marketing machines of the film, music, soft drink and clothing industries struggled to keep up, catching on to each new variety long after the kids had moved elsewhere, but by the '90s these business sectors were themselves being run by people who had grown up with Cool and knew its rules.

The other great change that the collapse of the '60s counter-culture wrought on Cool was to uncover a taste for darkness and violence which had always been latent but that the hippies had temporarily held at bay.

'60s radicals promoted revolutionary violence as both glamorous and justified, making Cool icons out of the AK-47 assault rifle, black beret and shades. Black Panther Eldridge Cleaver at a 1968 press conference in Los Angeles.

Even as far back as 1957 Norman Mailer could see that the personality of the hipster had a dark side that embraced simultaneously 'the inner life and the violent life, the orgy and the dream of love, the desire to murder and the desire to create'.[1] From the dark deeds of Charles Manson's 'Family' to the ultra-black comedies of Quentin Tarantino, these contradictions were to bloom during the next decades.

To Live Outside the Law You Must Be Honest

There have been many theories about what killed off '60s counter-culture but most agree that the initial idealism wore thin once it became clear that straight America was not about to 'turn on and drop out' en masse. Political radicals like the Weathermen became impatient and turned to terrorism, and violent and lumpen elements flocked into the 'movement' attracted by drugs and free sex. This in turn led to the relatively benign marijuana and acid favoured by most of the original participants being supplanted by amphetamines, cocaine and heroin, along with the violent criminals who imported them. All the while relentless low-level persecution by the police eroded general morale.

The alternative economy became absorbed back into the mainstream of business as major record companies bought up the independent labels that had sprung up since 1967 and turned the most popular acts into millionaires. The lifestyle that such wealth conferred on The Rolling Stones, The Who, Led Zeppelin, Rod Stewart, Jefferson Starship and Fleetwood Mac during the '70s created an image of Cool excess that provides a template to this day for musicians and their audiences. Like Hollywood moguls in previous decades, the rock stars adopted the

The 1970s were a decade of heroic dissipation, and many – like Gram Parsons (right) – did not survive it. Those who did, like Keith Richards (centre), created the template for succeeding generations of bad-boy rock stars. Also in this photo taken by Dominique Tarlé are Anita Pallenberg and Parsons's girlfriend Gretchen Burrel, at St-Jean Cap Ferrat, Provence, in 1971.

trappings of great wealth (country estates, smart cars, trophy spouses) but lacking old Hollywood's concern for privacy they made no attempt to conceal their debauchery: on the contrary, they flaunted it. Rather too many died from excess, but those who survived this decade of heroic abuse (the Keith Richardses and Iggy Pops) set a bad-boy benchmark for Cool, against which today's style commentators still measure their heroes – and often find them wanting.

The pornography industry rushed into the space for free sexual expression that the counter-culture had opened up by its anti-censorship efforts, and has now become one of largest earning sectors of the American economy. The sartorial styles of hippydom – long hair, sideburns, droopy moustaches, aviator shades, denim, mini-skirts and flared trousers – became the house style of urban lumpenproletariats and criminal underworlds across the globe, the uniform of every pimp, prostitute, dope dealer and television wrestler from Liverpool to Prague and Caracas to Manila. Not until the middle '90s was this style displaced by the baggies and trainers of hip-hop.

Gordon Burn, in his disturbing account of the life and crimes of the serial murderer Fred West describes the ghastly house at 25 Cromwell Street, Gloucester back in 1972 in these terms: 'An address that started getting handed around as a place where you could crash. Where the landlord [Fred West] was cool. No questions. There were many people around who wanted to belong to a house like that; to join an extended family.'[2] And sure enough, the accompanying photographs of West show the long sideburns and semi-Afro haircut of the '70s hippy manqué.

A great disillusionment set in among former counter-culture adherents, reflected in a profound cynicism that amounted to nihilism, towards any possibility of progressive political action. One way this nihilism expressed itself was through the cultivation of revenge fantasies: people began to dream of strong, armed heroes (not heroines until later) who would act out their fantasies of blowing away all the badness and

People began to dream of strong, armed heroes (not heroines until much later) who would act out their fantasies of blowing away all the badness and injustice in the world. Robert de Niro in Martin Scorsese's 1976 film *Taxi Driver*.

injustice in the world which the counter-culture had so signally failed to dislodge. The movie business, ever eager to please, reflected and reinforced this mood. For example in the mid-60s Clint Eastwood had become an unforgettable cult hero as 'The Man with No Name' of Sergio Leone's spaghetti Westerns, but in the disillusioned '70s he transformed himself into the vengeful cop Dirty Harry, of far more dubious political orientation. His catch-phrase 'Go on punk, make my day . . .' captured the essence of the new revenge-fantasy mindset. This nihilistic theme became steadily more exaggerated throughout the '70s, and more highly technologized. Violent mayhem and potently phallic hardware, of which Dirty Harry's .44 Magnum could be seen as the prototype, became symbols of getting even with one's tormentors, of tearing down the rotten world that you were powerless to alter in reality.

No Future

In parallel with this hardening of attitudes, the romantic, blues-based rock of Cream and Jimi Hendrix mutated into heavy metal, with its violent, macho and satanic iconography, which attracted a huge following of angst-ridden male adolescents. Toward the end of the '70s the punk movement arrived to gather all these dark and violent elements into a new synthesis. UK music historians tend to date the rise of punk from The Sex Pistols and their sub-Situationist Svengali, Malcolm McLaren, but there was already established in the USA a similar tradition of nihilistic and primitive rock, stretching from the '50s 'psychobillies' like Nervous Norvus, through '60s Latino 'garage' bands like The Standells to the arty nihilism of The Velvet Underground, The Stooges and The New York Dolls. Punk did for rock what Warhol had done for painting, dismissing the highly cultivated technique of '60s guitar heroes, and saying in effect 'anyone can do this'.

The movement that sprang up around this punk or new wave music tried to invert everything that the '60s counter-culture had stood for. Where the hippies had been largely apolitical, punk bands like The Clash and The Pop Group preached anarchist and Trotskyist revolution. Where hippies had worshipped the beauty of nature, punks revelled in ugliness. They shaved their heads into evermore extreme tonsorial structures to distance themselves from the coiffed quasi-hip look that was by now to be seen even on television newscasters. They adopted Carlsberg Special Brew and amphetamine sulphate as their drugs of choice in place of 'mellow' hashish and acid. The music was harsh, noisy and brutal in its sentiments, just as far from psychedelic as they could possibly get.

Punks even rejected what they saw as the hippies' obsession with sex, Johnny Rotten famously dismissing it as 'two minutes 50 seconds of squelching noises'. Punk also absorbed and adhered to a new feminism that was rising from the ashes of the counter-culture – the movement had many strong female figureheads like Siouxsie, Patti Smith, Polly Vinyl and Chrissie Hynde.

Punk, in the UK, left two important legacies which point in quite opposite directions. One was a new style of street-level anarchistic agitation which grew through the '80s and '90s – the anti-Poll Tax riots, the

Punk absorbed the new feminism rising from the ashes of the counterculture. The movement created many strong female figureheads, including Siouxsie, Patti Smith and Chrissie Hynde, shown here in 1981.

Animal Liberation Front's animal rights terrorism, New Age travellers, anti-highway campaigns – climaxing in the 1999 'Reclaim The City' riot. The other legacy was the 'style press', originating in punk fanzines that documented street styles, which trained up a whole generation of street-smart journalists who are now in positions of great influence on the colour supplements of the national dailies, and who have been chiefly instrumental in the '90s revival of Cool.

This may seem a curious development given that the punks had claimed to reject Cool and Hip along with Peace and Love, and professed to believe in nothing at all ('No Future', as The Sex Pistols's song would have it). However, this just serves to illustrate the dynamic by which Cool now mutates from generation to generation. It is difficult, some would say impossible, to maintain a Cool attitude once you become a parent and property owner (although millionaire rock stars try their best to have it both ways) and the punks were in reaction against the previous generation of ex-hippies who were crossing precisely that threshold into respectability. It was inevitable that the punks must reject the word 'cool' itself, as a despised reminder of their elder siblings' – even perhaps parents' – stoned ramblings, but nevertheless they themselves exhibited a structurally identical attitude of ironic defiance – only the vocabulary and haircuts had changed. It took barely more than a decade before a generation formed by punk found themselves media stars and could finally bring themselves to use the 'C' word.

Punk was of pivotal importance to the history of Cool and its mutations, for it created the template which all youth fashions since have worked from: invent a distinctive haircut and clothes, find a new drug and a new music (or maybe resurrect an old music), and you have a new movement. This formula has repeated itself from the '80s to today, from glam rock and the new romantics, through grunge to hip-hop, acid house, techno and trance. The subdivisions are becoming so subtle, the styles so evanescent that a whole industry has grown up just to track them.

Cool Violence

People have always been thrilled by images of violence and death, from the days of public hangings, through the Victorian 'penny dreadfuls', to the pre-war Hollywood Westerns, gangster movies and horror films, but during the '70s and '80s the emergence of Cool into mainstream society changed the way people consume such images. It's always been part of the liberal anti-censorship arguments to hold that teenagers in particular like to scare themselves witless with fictions (movies, computer games) because it makes their real-life anxieties look smaller: this is a theory of horrific art as Schadenfreude, that delight in other's misfortune that rejoices in the fact that it isn't happening to you. It is hard to escape from the impression, though, that for recent generations the relatively innocent satisfaction of Schadenfreude has begun to give way to straight-forward fantasy, that people are now reading horror film the same way they read pornography – 'I'm glad that's not happening to me' is being replaced by 'I wish I could do that'.

This change of attitude was begun by '60s radicals who promoted revolutionary violence as both glamorous and justified, making Cool icons of the AK-47 assault rifle and the black berets and shades of the Black Panthers. A paternalistic establishment had sought in the '50s to protect people from images of horror through censorship of horror movies and comics, but a left-wing anti-censorship movement opposed such censorship, seeing it as a colonial ruling class's attempt to conceal the violence that it perpetrates. Television coverage of the Vietnam War led a whole generation to view the world as a violent place (and the far greater violence that we know to have occurred in previous epochs offers little counterbalance since it is not on the nightly news).

Counter-culture film directors began depicting violence with a new realism, from Warren Beatty's *Bonnie and Clyde* to Sam Peckinpah's *The Wild Bunch*. Their work stimulated younger directors like John Carpenter,

Tobe Hooper and Abel Ferrara to venture with ever-greater audacity into the realms of hack and splatter, the 'watershed' perhaps being Tobe Hooper's *Texas Chainsaw Massacre*. Another powerful influence on the new mood was the boom in Kung Fu movies spawned in 1972 by the late Bruce Lee's *Fists of Fury*. These movies carried the powerful message that even the puniest of teenagers could trounce his tormentors by practising and applying an esoteric martial art, and by dint of their Asian settings and stars they packed a special charge for non-white teenagers all over the world – a short, slightly-built Chinese youth could smash the bad guys on screen, and become a rich Hollywood star in the real world.

The radical anti-censorship arguments had by now given way to the shrewd commercial observation that, particularly among teenage boys, extreme violence and cruelty was becoming deeply Cool.

Some post-punk factions began to embrace violent imagery, quasi-satanism and even elements of neo-Nazism as ways of proclaiming their hatred and disgust for *everything*. Early in Quentin Tarantino's *Pulp Fiction* Samuel L. Jackson's character terrifies a roomful of white petty criminals with his sermon from Ezekiel, providing the most perfect example of a new genre of 'hard-core revenge porn', and it is almost impossible (at least for a male) to watch this scene without, however briefly, being seduced or embarrassed by its brilliant depiction of raw power over others. A nihilistic teenager, embarrassed and enraged by his parents, school and teachers, anxious about sex (or lack of), humiliated by cleverer or richer peers, can project his tormentor's faces onto such screen victims, the modern equivalent of a voodoo priest sticking pins in a wax doll. Give him access to real firearms to act out the fantasy and you have the recipe for the recent rash of US school massacres, culminating at Columbine High School, Denver in April 1999.

Greed Is Good

The end of the '70s saw a sea change in the post-war economic and political consensus, with the election of right-wing governments, led, in 1979 in the UK by Margaret Thatcher's Conservatives, and in 1981 in the USA by Ronald Reagan's Republicans. These ideological allies, committed to the laissez-faire economics of the Chicago school, set about tearing down the Keynesian economic structures built up since the Second World War, attacking welfare programmes and promoting tax cuts for the creators (i.e. the possessors) of wealth. Thatcher and Reagan both proclaimed deeply conservative *social* policies like hard work, family values and a war on drugs, but by one of those delicious ironies of history their *economic* policies unleashed a hedonistic bacchanal that made the hippies look tame.

By preaching that individual enterprise was all important and social conscience unimportant they appealed to a greed for self-enrichment not seen since Guizot's *enrichissez-vous*. It had been considered not quite decent to flaunt wealth throughout the post-war period, and positively swinish in the radical '60s. Now tax cuts, deregulation and downsizing pumped huge amounts of money into the stock markets and increased the incomes of the young brokers and traders who worked there. The 'Young Upwardly-mobile Professional' or 'yuppy' was born. The yuppies combined a rampant individualism with hedonism and a taste for smart clothes, to create another mutant variant of Cool that was far closer to the style of the '50s originals than the hippies. If *One Flew Over the Cuckoo's Nest* captured the '60s spirit, then Oliver Stone's *Wall Street* did the same for the '80s, as Michael Douglas imbued the rapacious take-over merchant Gordon Gekko (whose line 'Greed is good' became the slogan of the era) with an intensity every bit as demonic as Jack Nicholson's McMurphy. If, as we believe, Cool always contains an element of rebellion, then the truth (unpalatable as it may be to left-wing sensibilities) is that the yuppies were revolting against precisely the collectivist, welfare-oriented consensus that had prevailed in both the USA and UK since the war. Real-life Gordon Gekkos such as Kirk Kerkorian and Michael Milliken were trying to smash the state, but this time it was the Welfare State. The yuppies of the '80s unleashed the fierce spirit of competition that lurks beneath the unruffled surface of Cool, and which the counter-culture, with its calls to drop out of the rat race, had vainly sought to suppress.

Cool Plays to Win

Nowhere was this elevation of competition to Cool status illustrated more clearly than in the profound change that overcame professional sport in the '80s. Back in the '50s sport in America had been the backbone of the college 'jock' culture, the province of crew-cut, conservative, intensely patriotic white males, and there was very little about it that could be considered Hip (Kerouac's early career as a college football star notwithstanding). The hipsters of that era preferred to direct their competitive urges instead into sexual conquest, honing their prowess in music (the beboppers) or writing (the beats). Personal appearance too became a game, with cutting contests for the slickest hair or the sharpest lapel, and even over-indulgence in alcohol and hard drugs had a competitive edge to it.

In contrast the sports stars of the time (for example World Heavyweight Boxing Champions Rocky Marciano and Floyd Patterson) tended to be reserved in speech and manner, and modest and self-effacing about their achievements: the prevailing code of ethics still emphasized fair-play and respect for your opponent as a moderator of the competitive urge, and the financial rewards were quite modest by today's standards. This state of affairs began to change in the '60s. Paul

Simon could sing plaintively (in his 1968 hit *Mrs. Robinson)* 'Where have you gone Joe Di Maggio?' to invoke a nostalgia for the sporting straightforwardness epitomized by the great baseball hero of the '50s, which Simon could already see was about to be lost.

Of course from its earliest days in West Africa a most important function of Cool has been to temper and moderate the aggressive instincts of the young male warrior, by transforming them into a nonchalant Cool pose that does not directly threaten, but equally does not betray weakness or passivity. In sport this function of Cool reflects itself in the way that the real stars make a seriously physically demanding activity appear to be a form of effortless play: the lightning moves of a

Michael Jordan walks on air. Cool in sport consists of making a seriously demanding activity appear to be a form of effortless play. Jordan jumped over Akeem Olajuwan to score at this 1988 NBA All-Stars game.

Muhammed Ali or a Sugar Ray Leonard; that apparent sixth sense for the killer pass or the strike at goal of soccer players like Maradona or Zidane; the legendary 'hang-time' of basketball star Michael Jordan which put the truth into Nike's brand-name 'Air Jordan'. This seeming effortlessness of technique, concealing a fierce underlying competitiveness, is what makes winning the ultimate Cool experience. Organized sport must always strike a fine balance between the narcissism inherent in perfecting the body and flaunting one's skills, and the subordination of individuality required for team work and painful training regimes. For much of this century Victorian ideas about the morally improving nature of these latter aspects had prevailed, but the hedonistic '60s shifted the balance: African-American sports stars, inspired by Ali's example, began to slip loose the bonds of American puritanism and to flaunt their technical skill with that sense of display and warrior-like passion that has been described as 'expressive styling'. Their white colleagues were quick to emulate the style – the whoops, the high fives, the dirty dancing in the endzone and all the rest of the Cool signifying.

In the '80s this new confidence in sport collided with the new competitiveness of the free marketeers in business, providing them with both the perfect metaphor for business prowess and a sartorial style far more suitable than the grey-flannel suit. Sportsmen and athletes in their track suits, baseball caps and trainers suggested a body image which was at the same time relaxed but powerful, and sportswear suddenly became both the height of Cool, and a hugely lucrative commercial enterprise. The sportswear industry exploded, inflating the salaries of sports personalities through sponsorship and aggressively marketing brands like Nike and Reebok by associating them with the biggest names. The result was a complete transmogrification of sport during the '90s with the athlete raised to super-celebrity, an icon of the untrammelled cult of the body (and dressed from head to toe in advertising logos). Indeed the marketing of sportswear remains the paradigm case of how an entire realm of action and experience can be transformed by commerce riding on the back of Cool.

The new competitive spirit in business and sport had combined to raise the cult of celebrity to undreamed heights, that were dubbed by Robert H. Frank and Philip J. Cook the *Winner Takes All Society* (New York, 1996). Certainly stars had always been Cool since the days of Elvis and Marilyn, and the counter-culture had done nothing to diminish their status: indeed The Beatles, The Stones and other bands took the cult to new heights. However, during the '80s boom the massively enhanced earning-power of screen and sport celebrities produced a paradoxical effect: these new stars were self-made and ostensibly more democratic than previous Hollywood élites – true popular heroes and heroines – but in reality their astonishing wealth permitted them to secede completely from ordinary society. This populist cult began to have a profound effect on the composition of the mass media. Starting from his bases in Australia and then the UK, Rupert Murdoch's News International set in train a process of 'tabloidization' of the mass-print media and later of television, whole sectors of which entirely abandoned the pursuit of news to follow the doings of this new pantheon: the Madonnas, Michael Jordans and Arnold Schwarzeneggers.

The early '80s also saw the founding of the personal computer industry which blossomed over the next two decades to become the USA's most important industrial sector, and in the process made Bill Gates the richest man in the world. Here too competition was all, and it became Cool to be ahead of the game, to be the smartest kid on the block. In stark contrast to the old data-processing industry (whose employees tended to wear tweed jackets with too many pens in the pocket) many pioneers of personal computing, such as the two Steves, Wozniak and Jobs, who founded Apple Computer were veterans of the counter-culture. Jobs had once hitch-hiked across India, while Wozniak was a rock musician and ex-phone freak (who in the '70s had designed the

'Blue Box' that let people make free long distance phone calls). Such men saw themselves as rebels out to smash monopolistic mini- and mainframe computer companies like IBM, whom they liked to depict in their advertising as totalitarian Big Brothers. Many of the young software and hardware engineers who founded this new industry speak the language of Cool, although in computing circles the word has evolved yet another nuance: a new technology can be described as 'cool' (maybe even 'way cool') if it is both elegant and truly innovative, the implication being that by recognizing its elegance you show yourself to be Cool – Cool technology confers Coolness on its user.

Straight outta Wall Street

In the USA street gangs, which had been sidelined during the counter-cultural events of the '60s, began to flourish again in the '80s, particularly in the Los Angeles area. A burgeoning drug culture controlled by gangs like the Bloods and the Crips brought new levels of violence to the streets with the 'drive-by' shooting. The drug of choice for the manic, money-making '80s had become cocaine because it gave you the energy to stay ahead in the new rat race, and because it cost so much that it announced you as a conspicuous consumer. Among Wall Street's young 'Masters of the Universe' a 'line or two' became as essential as a cup of coffee to get started in the morning. Street gangs moved in on this cocaine trade and turned it into very lucrative business, the more so after they introduced 'crack', a smokeable (as opposed to sniffable) free-base cocaine which was both cheaper and more addictive. Crack spread throughout the black areas of the USA like a plague destroying what little communal spirit was left in the neighbourhoods, while simultaneously enriching the gangs who sold it.

Just as the '50s street gang scene had given birth to doo-wop music,

Gangsta rap has been enthusiastically adopted by youth of all colours, classes and nations. Songs about beating on 'hos and bitches are guaranteed to upset mums and dads who grew up with 'All You Need Is Love'. Run DMC in 1987.

so this resurgent gang life of the '80s created a new musical genre, hip-hop or rap, as pioneered by Kool Herc, Grandmaster Flash, Afrika Bambaataa and the Sugarhill Gang. Like doo-wop this new style was based on vocal abilities rather than instrumental virtuosity, consisting of rhythmic declamation of lyrics over the backing of an existing dance record. As with punk, the fact that it did not require proficiency on a musical instrument made hip-hop highly democratic, and it spread throughout the world with a rapidity and breadth that punk had never achieved.

Musically hip-hop was the culmination of a trend in black music to pare down the melody and emphasize the rhythm which started with James Brown and Sly Stone in the '60s, and evolved through '70s disco-funk. In hip-hop the recently perfected drum machine replaced human drummers, bass synthesizers replaced the bass player, and sampling and 'scratching' existing dance records added complexity to the rhythm.

As the '80s wore on the attitudes behind hip-hop became equally pared down: from the good-time 'boogie down' sentiments of disco towards a celebration of sexual violence, firearms and wealth in acts like

Ice Cube and Snoop Dogg. Gold chains and Uzis became new symbols of Cool to replace black berets and AK-47s. Despite a veneer of revolutionary, anti-police talk, this hip-hop attitude was perfectly in tune with the '80s pursuit of fame, money and sex by 'whatever means necessary'. By the end of the decade a gunshot wound had become the leading cause of death for young black males in several US cities, and later in the '90s the violence started claiming the rap stars themselves, either as targets, like Tupac Shakur and Biggie Smalls, or through incarceration, like Snoop Dogg.

Given the new fascination with violence it's hardly surprising that gangsta rap has been enthusiastically adopted by white youth of all classes and all nations as a stick with which to beat their parent's generation – songs about beating on 'hos and bitches, are pretty well guaranteed to upset mums and dads who grew up with 'All You Need Is Love'. But of course this is not quite such a clear-cut reversal as it may seem, because more than 30 years ago the authors' generation were identifying in a similar way with the only slightly less macho lyrics of Muddy Water's 'Mannish Boy'.

Rave On

By the mid-90s Cool had mutated into dozens of very different-looking styles – the baggy garb of the ragga could hardly be further from the bebopper's sharp suit, or Jimi Hendrix's frilly shirt. Their vocabularies have changed too – substituting 'phat' for 'far out', or 'diss' for 'put down' – but none of this should blind us to the fact that the underlying concerns of Cool are always the same, to maintain respect and pursue one's pleasure by observing the right codes of appearance and behaviour.

The history of popular culture is one of cross-fertilization. Just as black R&B crossed the Atlantic after the Second World War to nurture

The Beatles and The Stones, and then re-crossed in the '60s to re-fertilize American rock, so hip-hop came back across the Atlantic and spawned myriad new forms of electronic dance music in Europe during the late '80s and '90s. These rave and dance cultures have captured the imaginations of new generations, and given fresh impetus to the spread of Cool. Nowadays a dance style can cross and re-cross the Atlantic (or the Mediterranean, or the Pacific) in a matter of weeks rather than years.

Perhaps the greatest achievement of a generation of politically-correct school teachers has been to make colour disappear as an issue among Cool youth. The Beastie Boys, The Wu Tang Clan, Black Grape: who can tell what's black and what's white any more? (If the infamous murder of Steven Lawrence in London shows us that racism still exists in the UK, the public revulsion also shows how far beyond the pale it now is.) In fact in putting hip-hop together with the new status of black sports stars like Michael Jordan and Mike Tyson, Cool has suddenly started to look like a black thing all over again.

One thing that is different in this latest pass through the cross-fertilization cycle is that the mass media and advertising industries are no longer behind the game. They can no longer tolerate a five-year time lag while the old farts at head office frantically recruit youth scouts for the latest fashion. Cool has become the official language of advertising and entertainment for teenagers, up through 'middle youth' and all the way to Mick-Jagger-age. Perhaps only the over-sixties are nowadays perplexed by the psychedelic Pot Noodle ads, by Flat Eric, or by those comedians who've applied so much ironic spin that they become straight again.

The board rooms of major media corporations are now filled with people who freaked out in the '60s but got enterprising in the '80s, and they understand perfectly what they are seeing and hearing, while their thirty-something directors are out there clubbing, doing Es and lines with their target audience. Richard Benson, in *Arena* magazine (March 1999) identified a new class of young business people he calls 'flexecutives' who make big money designing web sites, advising marketeers about youth preferences, organizing events and gallery shows.[3] They have no fixed job but rather a number of 'projects'; they have no deep belief in anything except in their own hipness and their recreations are snorting cocaine and travelling the world in search of 'authenticity' and 'spirituality': the perfect portrait of '90s Cool.

CHAPTER SIX

The Look of Cool

The essence of Cool has always been, first of all, to look Cool. From the razor-sharp suits of the Kray twins in David Bailey's '60s portraits to the wrap around mirror shades of a late '90s clubber, Cool always manifests a deep concern with its appearance. Sometimes this concern may spill over into excess and exaggeration – the foppish frills of the New Romantic or the flashing gold chains of the rapper – but more typically the look of Cool is obtained subtly through distinctive body language, a leisurely rolling gait, a meticulously chosen hat or hairstyle, a mute expression and an air of circumspection. Such a concern with appearance felt quite revolutionary in the '50s precisely because it was so deeply at odds with the prevailing work ethic, which emphasized self improvement, sobriety and a self-denying sartorial uniformity where what mattered was to find a suit sufficiently anonymous that you would 'blend in' and look like a 'regular guy'. The carefully-coiffed hair of Cool teenagers from Elvis onwards was a source of outrage to the parental generation (both in the capitalist West and far more so in the dour socialist bloc) as it was felt to be at once unpatriotic and possibly effeminate.

Much of the look of modern Cool was prefigured by 19th-century dandies like the comte Robert de Montesquiou, portrayed by Giovanni Boldoni in 1897.

As is so often the case, such prejudice revealed underlying elements of truth. Cool's visual sensibility may well ultimately derive from African notions of personal display that lie outside the tradition of European puritanism with its emphasis on modesty and plainness of speech and dress. Similarly there is something in the look of Cool that flouts established conventions of Western masculinity, and may appear closer to some conventional notions of the feminine. Feminist art critics such as Laura Mulvey have employed concepts from Freudian and Lacanian psychoanalysis to theorize ways of looking in visual culture, and in particular the 'gaze', with its connotation of a long ardent look. In particular the 'male gaze' is analysed as an aggressive and possessive act, 'the publicly-sanctioned actions of a peeping Tom'[1] which treats its female recipient as an inanimate object of desire. Cool, in its strongest forms, radically abandons that kind of male gaze. The glance – rather than the gaze – of Cool is consciously drained of visible desire, just as in popular parlance to take 'a cool look' at something means to approach it undistorted by passion or emotion. Cool does not gaze *at* others, but appears *to* others: it does not gaze but wishes to be gazed at. That does not mean that the Cool glance is passive, but rather detached – it expresses an indifference that challenges the other to attempt to attract its interest.

There is no better place to examine the look of Cool at work than in Hollywood movies, because they not only depict Cool but have played a major role in its creation. For 50 years the screen presences of Humphrey Bogart and Lauren Bacall, Marlene Dietrich, James Dean, Marlon Brando, Robert Mitchum, Paul Newman, Dennis Hopper, John Travolta, Sharon Stone, and scores of others have defined Cool for the rest of

For most, Cool is a posture that must be worked on; for a very few, it is in the bones. Marlene Dietrich (1901–1992).

Cool's glance – rather than gaze – is consciously drained of visible desire, just as in popular parlance to take 'a cool look' at something means to approach it undistorted by emotion. Cool does not gaze at others but appears to others; it does not gaze but wishes to be gazed at. Brando c. 1961.

us. One could strike populist attitudes by claiming that these are mere actors, and that they 'stole' their Cool look from the streets, but that would not be very productive, and only partially true, for from the beginning of mass cinema-going, film stars have given back to the street at least as much as they found there (in Cool if not in hard currency).

If asked to select one exemplar from among these Cool images, we could hardly do better than pick the deadpan screen presence of Robert Mitchum. Whether playing the relatively benign Philip Marlowe in *Farewell My Lovely*, the malignant psychopath of *Cape Fear* or the mad preacher of *Night of the Hunter*, Mitchum always successfully conveyed the impression of a man whose ties to Western Civilization were frayed down to a single thread, an effect that owed as much to his appearance as to his acting, effective though it was. With his sleepy 'don't care' eyes and a barely perceptible permanent smirk (a feature he shares with Bill Clinton: make of that what you will) he exudes a combination of unflappability and slight aloofness that recall the original dictionary definition of 'cool'. A Mitchum character always hints at amorality and unpredictability, with a powerful competitive streak that borders on the anti-social and which is in rebellion against domesticity and *petit bourgeois* complacency. There is the deep, but subtle and unflashy, concern with appearance: the correct tilt of a hat or cut of a collar, complete with an attitude of ironic detachment that can always produce an astringent witticism in the face of great danger. Finally, and above all, there appears to be a barely constrained capacity for pleasure which the audience senses would probably be of a kind and intensity they have never experienced themselves.

Mitchum is one of the best examples of a Cool Hollywood actor who essentially plays himself, not in the sense that he truly is the psychopath from *Cape Fear*, but rather that his real-life personality provides the necessary resources, such as the suggestion of danger and recklessness, that lesser method actors might have to torment themselves for weeks to summon up. Jack Nicholson and Dennis Hopper are the other actors that spring to mind as possessing this quality. Mitchum is famous for his self-deprecating interviews in which he belittles both his skill as an actor and the quality of his movies, while expressing no regrets about his drinking, the time he spent in jail for drug possession, and other louche escapades. A typically laconic quip is, 'I started out to be a sex fiend but I couldn't pass the physical'. Since the Hollywood gossip rags adored this kind of stuff, some might argue that Mitchum was doing no more than feeding them what they wanted to hear to build up a Cool reputation, but that scarcely matters – a film star is as Cool as the parts he plays, on or off the screen.

Is it possible to isolate those traits that make actors like Mitchum and the roles they play Cool? Is it possible to expose what Bogart and Bacall in

With his sleepy 'don't care' eyes and barely perceptible permanent smirk, Robert Mitchum's characters always hint at amorality and unpredictability.

To Have and Have Not, Newman in *Hud*, Travolta and Thurman in *Pulp Fiction* and Michael Caine in *Get Carter* have in common? We would suggest that it is the strong sense of self that is conveyed, the impression that these are their own men and women, beholden to no institution and not even perhaps to the law itself. It is a misconception often employed in comic parodies like Henry Winkler's The Fonz in the television series *Happy Days*, that to be Cool means the suppression of emotional display. What Cool actually refuses is the sentimental or incontinent display of negative emotions – parental wrath, patriotic fervour, moral outrage – which are the very definition of Uncool. However, Cool respects intense passion, and from some angles the look of Hollywood Cool is merely a mask covering an extreme form of romanticism, which, so the dictionary tells us, involves 'an emphasis on feeling and content rather than order and form, on the sublime, supernatural, and exotic, and the free expression of the passions and individuality'. In short, Cool economizes on emotion rather than suppressing it altogether, preferring the bitter-sweet varieties, those emotions it deems to be both intense and unconventional.

A Cool Aesthetic

In the visual arts Abstract Expressionism is the school that most people would associate with Cool, if only because it has become a cliché among movie and television drama makers to use the works of, for example, Jackson Pollock or Mark Rothko over a cool Miles Davis jazz soundtrack to typify the classic period of Cool. But was Abstract Expressionism actually Cool? In fact, what could it mean to say that a painting, or a style of painting is Cool? It is certainly a judgement one could make about the artist as a person, and indeed Jackson Pollock might serve as the textbook example of the self-destructive strain of Cool personality: obsessive, alcoholic, sexually competitive and suicidally dangerous behind a steering wheel. But does that necessarily make the look of his paintings Cool too? Some art critics are currently applying the term 'cool hedonism' to describe the lightness of the paintings of Matisse, and hence their renewed popularity as against those of Picasso. But would anyone describe Henri Matisse the man as Cool?

We have so far defined Cool as a relation to society, a form of private rebellion; so one could perhaps call representational paintings Cool if the subject matter they depict is Cool – for example if they depict low-life and deviance like the works of Otto Dix or George Grosz – or if they merely, as in the work of Alex Katz, depict Cool-looking people. For example, a 1996 retrospective show, self-consciously named *Birth of the Cool* after the seminal Miles Davis album, collected together '50s artists including Pollock, Rothko and Katz, and reassessed them in precisely this context, as reflecting Cool values. According to the catalogue these consist of taking an 'elementary, alert and existential stand. Cool is emotional but controlled, serious and detached, matter-of-fact, and unpretentious'.[2] The catalogue went on to hail Alex Katz's inscrutable self-portrait as the coolest self-portrait in history, and it is true that the impassive face under the pork-pie hat, button-down shirt and slim tie speak volumes about the body language of Cool in the early '60s.

But can the term Cool really be applied to abstract paintings, particularly to those of Pollock, some of which appear impassioned, if not frenzied? Actually this is not a significant contradiction. Cool does not refuse to express all emotions, only the ones it considers sentimental or commonplace. Expressionism was not an empty name: the Abstract Expressionists were doing, with typically American pragmatism, what French existentialists were only theorizing about, and that was trying to communicate instantaneous existential states – the process which Norman Mailer (speaking about jazz) summed up as 'I feel this, and now you do too'. Abstract Expressionism represented an individualized revulsion away from political radicalism in art, in favour of individual salvation through intensity of experience, which places it centrally within that Cool sensibility that we have described as a consequence of disgust at the horrors of the Second World War and anxieties of the Cold War. Recent revelations that the CIA used Abstract Expressionism in its propaganda war against the collectivist culture of the Soviet union suggests that those spooks – mostly Ivy-League-educated – may have been running some way ahead of public taste, but they were definitely not mistaken in recognizing that this art expressed a new brand of confident individualism to which Eastern bloc populations would soon begin to aspire, in secret.

Abstract Expression and post-bop jazz exhibited a certain unity of visual and musical styles that was at the time experienced as modern, as in 'modern art' and 'modern jazz'. From an art historical point of view, the high point of Modernism had long-since passed, and more importantly, the high Modernism of the years immediately preceding and following the First World War had largely passed the 'man in the street' by. Indeed the Modernism of Schoenberg in music, Picasso, Klee *et al.* in painting, Eliot, Pound and Joyce in letters had signalled an abandonment by artists of a concern with the tastes of a mass audience. In the nineteenth century a radical clerk might have appreciated Dickens or Zola, but few of them would care for Pound's *Cantos*, *Pierrot Lunaire*, or the *Les Demoiselles d'Avignon*. It is therefore not stretching things too far to see '50s Cool aesthetics as popular culture catching up with Modernity – it was, if you like 'the people's Modernism'. Cool started to be appreciated as an aesthetic style, if not yet a life style, by many thousands of people who still lived conventional lives centred on work and family, but felt dissatisfied with the bland commercialized culture of the times. During the '60s the innovations of Abstract Expressionism and other 'modern' styles would find their way, suitably diluted, into Swedish kitchen utensils, colourful plastic furniture and the formica tabletops of a million burger joints.

However, what Abstract Expressionism still shared with high Modernism was the notion of the painter as someone who stood apart from the everyday world, pursuing a personal vision that involved the mastery of certain techniques. The popular press at the time may have mocked Abstract Expressionist 'action painting' with the suggestion that anyone, a child (or even a monkey) could do it. However, those who attempted to replicate a Pollock or a Rothko quickly discovered that enormous aesthetic judgement and technical skill is involved. In this sense Abstract Expressionism was not Cool because it still believed that art mattered, it cared for and respected the artistic project. However, in a different sense it was as Cool as those Italian courtiers of the Renaissance who cultivated *sprezzatura*, the art of making the difficult appear effortless.

Jackson Pollock was one of the last great figures of a Western art tradition that stretches back to the Middle Ages. First there was the artist as provider and keeper of the community's religious imagery, then the artist as hired chronicler of bourgeois wealth and success, and at the last the artist as romantic rebel, pursuing new ways of seeing untainted by the needs of commerce. Pre-war radical art movements – starting with Duchamp and Dada and passing through Surrealism to the Situationist International – saw that this tradition had already ended, that art had 'died', but the problem was that no-one else seemed to notice and people kept on painting anyway. Kandinsky and Picasso, despite the fact that they painted for themselves in the first instance, retained the belief that art had the power to have effects in and on society. In the '60s, with the coming of Pop Art, that belief died and art finally made its peace with capitalism. It became a deadpan celebration of popular culture, and never more so than when it appeared to be at its most shocking and transgressive. This, rather than Abstract Expressionism, was the true 'Cooling' of art.

Warhol and Factory Art

When in the '60s the former Abstract Expressionist Jasper Johns started to paint the American flag and make bronze beer cans, or Roy Lichtenstein made paintings in the language of comic strips, they were still posing questions about the relationship between high art and familiar mass-produced images. In using the ephemera of consumer society as material for visual representation they were still working a territory first mapped by Dada and the ready-mades of Marcel Duchamp.

It took the ambiguous influence of Andy Warhol to move art on to quite new territory, and in the process to put Cool firmly in the saddle. A successful commercial artist with avant-garde pretensions, it was Warhol who first understood that bourgeois high culture could be subverted by

Andy Warhol in New York *c. 1967*. It is impossible to overestimate Warhol's significance in the history of Cool; he completed the job started by Elvis, giving popular culture the confidence to cast off any remaining deference to the aesthetic achievements of high art.

making it easier rather than more difficult as the high Modernists had once believed. Subverted not to any revolutionary end, but nevertheless to a demotic one, for Warhol's adoration of celebrity, stardom and wealth was actually in tune with the egalitarian spirit of the times. The post-war Cool aesthetic may have been forged in the cinema, but Warhol, whether consciously or not it scarcely matters, divined that this star system was quite as 'élitist' as any branch of bourgeois high art, since it still depended on exceptional good looks and some notion of acting talent. He ruthlessly stripped away at least the latter requirement from his own movies. As Warhol was to put it, 'I only wanted to find great people and let them be themselves and talk about what they usually talk about and I'd film them for a certain length of time and that would be the movie.'[3] It was but a short step to the sound bite that became the nearest thing to his manifesto: 'In the future, everyone will be famous for fifteen minutes.'

Far from turning Hollywood stars into sacred icons, Warhol reduced them to commodities, and not in a critical but in an approving way, for

Warhol loved the consumer democracy that the USA had become, and wanted to express its spirit by democratizing art, by removing all the difficulty from it: 'What's great about this country is that America started the tradition where the richest consumers buy essentially the same thing as the poorest (sic). You can be watching TV and see Coca-Cola and you know that the President drinks Coke, Liz Taylor drinks Coke, and just think, you can drink Coke, too. A Coke is a Coke and no amount of money can get you a better Coke than the one the bum on the corner is drinking.'[4]

Warhol, like previous Pop artists, elevated the ephemera of consumer society such as the famous Campbells soup cans, to the status of already-art, but he removed all their hidden meanings – he sampled and copied, but without the satirical intent of Dada or Surrealism. Where Duchamp had imbued his pioneering works with a 'difficult' irony, a Warhol just came with a bland 'here it is, isn't it cool'. Where Jasper Johns had insisted on reworking the mundane through the techniques and materials of high art, Warhol used household distemper and delegated its application to assistants: his message was that anyone could do this. Where Dada and Surrealism had failed to topple high art, Warhol and his followers succeeded by reducing it to a matter of decoration and personal taste. Anyone can 'understand' a Warhol Marilyn.

This is not to suggest that Warhol lacked irony, but his was irony of an altogether Cooler, less political, more knowing variety. The irony implicit in radical art from Dada onwards fed off a tension between the ideals of romanticism and the brutal history and politics of the early-twentieth century: a recognition that art could no longer have any function but to shock the bourgeoisie. Warholian irony concealed not tension but acceptance. It said yes, consumer society is lazy and shallow, but that's OK – we can play with it, colour it in like a colouring book (and we can make lots of money from it, and that's Cool too). Cynicism turned itself inside out, into a democratic cynicism, the cynicism of the people themselves. Any residual awe or deference toward seriousness of artistic purpose that might have survived in the populace was punctured for ever, as was the notion of art that has content, or makes social statements.

Warhol saw clearly that anxiety, not poverty, was the new enemy; that anxiety was caused by change; and that the cure for anxiety was Cool stasis:

> I could never stand to watch all the most popular action shows on TV, because they're essentially the same plots and the same shots and the same cuts over and over again. Apparently, most people love watching the same basic thing, as long as the details are different. But I'm just the opposite: if I'm going to sit and watch the same thing I saw the night before, I want it to be essentially the same, because the more you look at the exact same thing, the more the meaning goes away, and the better and emptier you feel.[5]

David Sylvester adds by way of comment that this represents a journey 'from Pop to Zen.' Perhaps he should have said from Pop to ultimate Cool. It has even been reported recently (*The Observer* 14 March 1999) that Warhol may have suffered from the mild form of autism called Asperger Syndrome, which would explain his love of repetition and lack of emotional depth, but if that is the case then there must be a widespread epidemic of the syndrome for his attitude echoes powerfully through all the art that has been made since the '60s.

Post-Warholian irony has not only become the safe road into an artistic career, as witness Jeff Koons, Damien Hirst and BritArt, but it also provides fodder for the theory mills of post-modernist critics by apparently justifying their belief in the collapse of all meanings. It is impossible to overestimate the significance of Warhol to the history of Cool: he completed the job started by Elvis Presley, finally giving popular culture the confidence to cast off any remaining deference to the aesthetic achievements of high art. Since Warhol, art has been about attitude and not artefacts. With his defiantly artificial blonde wig and huge spectacles, Warhol understood that in the age of celebrity worship the artist's persona becomes the work, and that whatever artefacts he (or increasingly she) produces matter only as outward signs of an inwardly Cool attitude. A generation raised on Warholian aesthetics now controls the levers of popular culture in the television, record and movie industries, and they are slurping down what remains of high bourgeois culture like a thick milk-shake. All that was needed to complete the rout was for a couple of inspired hippies to invent the board game 'Trivial Pursuit', providing a format through which both Scholarship and Art could be effortlessly absorbed into 'show business'.

Warhol's musical protégés The Velvet Underground, after languishing in incomprehension for a decade, were rediscovered by the punks and became a dominant influence on all subsequent popular music, supplying that element of intellectual nihilism needed to complement the energy and sensuality inherited from black music. Warhol's 'postcards from hell', sombre road accidents and electric chairs presented without comment or compassion, set the tone for a mockingly sadistic sensibility that is now to be seen everywhere from Tarantino to the bad-boy brothers Chapman, whose reworkings of Goya's *Horrors of War* and mutant children attempt, in their own elegant words, 'to rub salt into your inferiority complex, smash your ego in the face, gouge your eyes from their sockets and piss in the empty holes'. Pretending not to be Cool can be Cool too, especially if you can sell the posture for ten grand a throw.

We are still living through the consequences of Warhol's vision of a democratized Cool – a garish outpouring of kitsch, voyeurism and exhibitionism that constitutes contemporary popular culture, from Yoof TV and satellite porn to *Hello* magazine. Warhol sniffed out the narcissism that lies at the heart of Cool, banished its passion and intelligence and encouraged Pop culture to fall in love with itself, free from any taint of real feeling or critical thought. We may all be stars now, but stars who have been brought down to earth.

The Cool Vernacular

Warhol finally destroyed the boundaries of 'fine art' that Dada had merely shaken, by extending them to encompass kitsch. But where then does Cool fit within the original, uninterpreted realm of popular artefacts from which Warhol drew his inspiration? At several points in our account so far we have touched on the importance, for example, of dress codes and haircuts in distinguishing the Cool from the great Uncool, but we have not so far given much in the way of concrete examples. That is a deliberate choice, not because we feel such details are in any way beneath our concern, but because there already exists a vast body of literature that describes the content of what we might term 'popular Cool aesthetics': that body is of course the style and fashion press, whose sole *raison d'être* is to document the ins and outs, twists and turns of this aesthetic. There are whole books, for example, devoted to the history of the black leather jacket, the white tee-shirt, the blue jean and other iconic items of Cool clothing.

We are more interested in whether there is a deeper structure lying within this mass of ever-changing details concerning trouser-leg widths, collar points and hair partings, something that might unite the besuited bebopper with the pump-action trainer of the hip-hopper. In fact it does appear that there are two quite opposite structuring principles balancing one another within the popular aesthetic of Cool, one being an obsessive and often subtle concern with detail and decoration, and the other being a competitive urge to gigantism, to make everything bigger, faster, longer, shinier, louder. This second impulse can be understood as a deliberate inversion of the bourgeois virtue of moderation, so that almost any excess is often seen as Cool.

As an example of the first tendency, we could devote a whole chapter to say, the way that the laces of trainers have been worn by hip-hoppers over the last decade. Each style is a matter of exquisite importance at the time – get it wrong and you are out – but new styles replace each other with great rapidity, and also vary from city to city and country to country. A similar concern for subtle detail can be seen over shirt collars among the '50s beboppers (Billy Eckstine was almost as famous for the roll-collar shirt he invented as for his singing) or over the size of turn-ups on blue jeans among '70s British skinheads.

The countervailing force, a competitive impulse toward gigantism can also be seen at work in clothes fashions (for example, the '40s zoot suit, the ragga's baggies) and in haircuts (the long hair of the hippy, the exploding '70s Afro, the punk's Mohican), but it is perhaps best demonstrated by its affect on motor vehicles. The archetypal example is the chopped motorcycle or chopper, which began life as the plain Harley Davidson, ridden by generations of American policemen, but evolved, like the beaks of Darwin's finches, into a myriad bizarre forms: with outrageously extended forks and 'ape-hanger' handlebars, acres of chrome and evermore ornate and grotesque paintings on the petrol tank. In the chopper you can see both the contrary tendencies at work: the stretching to make the forks longer than the next guys', but also the obsessive micro-detailing, for example, tiny American eagles engraved on each chromed bolt head. A similar study could be made of the evolution and taxonomy of the hot-rod car, and its meaning to its owner.

It could be objected that this scheme ignores that minimalist wing of Cool aesthetics which values simplicity and a lack of adornment, and certainly there was once (perhaps prior to 1990) a clear distinction between such a 'high' Cool, which derives directly from the Modernist

Two structuring principles oppose one another within the popular Cool aesthetic: an obsessive, often subtle concern with decoration and a competitive urge to make things bigger, faster, longer, shinier, louder. In art-historical terms, this opposition most closely approaches the Baroque sensibility.

design traditions of Scandinavia and Bauhaus, and a vernacular or street Cool on the basis of the social class of their consumers as much as their aesthetics. However, since the Pop revolution wrought by Warhol and others, this distinction is becoming more and more difficult to maintain: one is as likely to see an inner-city crack dealer driving a black Porsche 911 and a television executive riding a custom-painted Harley, as the reverse. Cool has become uneasy with any system of aesthetic judgement, and to declare something a 'design classic' is to risk thereby making it Uncool. What is more, on closer examination of the minimalist, one may well discover that they are simply vying to be matter and blacker than the next, and just as competitive as any Puerto Rican low-rider.

If asked to situate the vernacular Cool aesthetic within the broader framework of art history, then its twin emphases on the spectacular and the minutely decorated would tempt one to see it as being closest to the sensibility of Baroque. The original seventeenth–eighteenth century Baroque style served both as Catholicism's aesthetic weapon against Protestant austerity during the religious wars of the Reformation, and as a means for the nobility to conspicuously flaunt their wealth and power, which is almost too neat a fit for the overall thesis of this book; which is that modern Cool represents both a rejection of the Protestant Work Ethic and an adaptation to competitive consumerism.

CHAPTER SEVEN

Cool Relations

Cool conquered post-war Hollywood not merely as an aesthetic category but as a sensibility well-suited to the lives of a new, virtualized aristocracy: those media moguls who no longer own the land we live on, but rather the landscape of our imaginations. Cool is the ideal sensibility for anyone who must live by constant self-reinvention, never forming any permanent bonds. An industry whose whole basis lay in manufacturing celebrity and exploiting sexuality was unlikely to retain the stern moralities of Protestant Christianity or Orthodox Judaism for long, despite gestures toward conventional morality like the Hayes Code.

Where old Hollywood magnates had been masters of creative hypocrisy, preaching morality to the peasants while organizing orgies in the Blue Room, in the '60s Hollywood abandoned such pretence and what was once confined to the casting couch came into the open (often literally). Similarly, where the image of non-committal Cool sex portrayed by Bogart and Bacall in the '40s and '50s had been mostly a dramatic device – in their real life Bogart and Bacall had a passionate and committed relationship – by the late '60s non-committal Cool sex was the norm

The noncommittal Cool sex portrayed by Bogart and Bacall was mostly a dramatic device – in real life, they had a passionate and committed relationship.

for the new generation of Warren Beatty, Jack Nicholson and the rest. It would not be too long before the masses began to imitate their 'betters', and Cool became the attitude to cultivate if you wanted to score . . .

There is an excellent portrait of the calculating and instrumental nature of this new Cool promiscuity in Peter Biskind's account of the love life of the late Hal Ashby (perhaps the hippest of the New Hollywood directors): 'You could predict when the girlfriends would come into his life, and when they were going to leave his life. When he was in post-production, getting rid of a movie, he would be getting rid of his relationships. His old friend or girlfriend would be leaving, and he would have struck up a relationship with somebody new.' Ashby's own description of his behaviour is more succinct: 'When one's gone, you just open the window, there's another one climbing right in.'[1]

The influence of Hollywood was only one, if important, determinant of the so-called 'sexual revolution' that swept through Western societies in the '60s and '70s as they finally left behind nineteenth-century repressive sexual mores. The 1974 book *Hot & Cool Sex: Cultures in Conflict* by Anna and Robert Francouer examines some of these causes, from a viewpoint that was very much of the time, portraying the new Cool sexuality as a real revolution: equally fun and equally beneficial to both genders. In a curious blend of scholarly treatise and political manifesto the Francoeurs counterpoise egalitarian Cool sex against what they term the possessiveness, role-stereotyping, aggressive chauvinism and competitiveness of a 'hot sex culture', seeking 'The restoration and maturation of male–female relations to equal partnership without sex stereotypes and fixed roles, and the overthrowing of the fear-motivated segregation of human sexuality in everyday life.'[2] A revived feminist movement that had grown up on the political fringes of the counter-culture also tried to see things in this light, for a while.

The Francoueurs usefully identify the material pre-conditions for the spreading of Cool sex. Foremost was a crucial demographic factor, the growth of the single population. Between 1960 and 1972 the number of single adults in the USA doubled, from 20 million out of 116 million adults in 1960 to over 40 million out of 139 million in 1972 (although we would have liked information about how many of these were widows and pensioners). Next came the decline during the '60s of religious morality and Victorian abstinence, as evidenced by surveys showing the prevalence of pre-marital sexual intercourse among college students, coupled with the easy availability of birth control measures which made possible 'the separation of sexual intercourse from procreation'. The raising of the school leaving age (in Britain in 1974) extended the period of adolescent dependence, and '60s counter-culture ideas, conveyed particularly by rock musicians, helped promulgate the desirability of Cool sex. But the Francoeurs also saw that another material change was required before Cool sex could prevail: 'the economic independence of women is indispensable for any move away from Hot Sex patriarchy'.[3]

The dysfunctional aspects of Cool sex are more visible in our post-AIDS era than they were to the Francoeurs. What they saw as a quest for sexual authenticity in 'becoming more fully human', has in practice degenerated into a flight from feeling, from the messiness of real intimacy into the sleazy world of the casual sexual encounter, the quickie divorce and the 'non-possessive' relationship, and it has been accompanied not

The sexual revolution that swept through Western societies in the 1960s and '70s sought at first to overthrow repressive 19th-century mores, counterpoising egalitarian Cool sex against the possessiveness, role-stereotyping and competitiveness of the steamy old hot sex culture. Jeanne Moreau and Henri Serre in François Truffaut's 1962 film *Jules et Jim*.

by a lessening but rather an intensification of sexual competition. Each generation since the '60s has reinvented Cool sex in its own preferred image (in the case of the punks even pretending not to like it), pushing the boundaries ever further out, so that today sado-masochism, body piercing and fetishism are flaunted to shock the older generations of ex-hippies. Cool sex is still largely a young persons' game but it exhibits a rather alarming persistency. Sampling Cool sex in youth would seem very often to be the psychological highpoint of a life, beyond which no further personal development is possible or desirable. Survivors of the '60s generation are now approaching retirement age, but as the Jagger divorce demonstrates some of them still manage to put it about like teenagers – and those young people who profess to be sickened by the spectacle may actually admire them in secret and hope one day to emulate them. For most people, however, keeping up the Cool façade for life proves too debilitating, and can all too easily descend into bathos. The ageing hippy stud is becoming a tragi-comic figure, and those who once bravely broke sexual taboos may wind up only with a place in the pantheon of 'great eccentrics'.

Cool and Gender

By the '70s feminists had recognized that they were getting a raw deal from the new Cool sex, and moved into other territories, becoming for example pro-censorship. Does this mean that Cool is a gendered phenomenon? Are women as Cool as men? Do they want to be?

Certainly there are now, and have been for centuries, women capable of keeping up with any man in drinking, drug abuse and promiscuity – one thinks immediately of Billie Holiday, Janis Joplin and Nico (to confine ourselves to the safely dead). Hollywood has provided plenty of fictional Cool heroines who are more than a match for their male equivalents,

There have been many Cool women, including Billie Holiday, who were more than a match for the men in drinking, drug abuse and promiscuity. However, Holiday's biography suggests that she was even more damaged emotionally by her 'on-the-edge' way of life than her male contemporaries.

as displayed by Lauren Bacall versus Bogart, Kathleen Turner versus Nicholson, Barbara Stanwyck versus anyone, and by Linda Fiorentino's extraordinary performance in *The Last Seduction*.

For a contemporary example one need look no further than Hillary Rodham Clinton, whose ability to retain her Cool in the face of the most extraordinary provocations has been witnessed by all America. Washington journalists have even coined a term, her 'battle mouth', for that determined but unruffled facial expression she deploys in the aftermath of each fresh Bill embarrassment, and there is much anecdotal evidence that this demeanour conceals a ferocious temper (which has of course been the primary function of Cool, from the warriors of ancient Benin onwards).

Are examples like these sufficient evidence that Cool is a gender-neutral phenomenon, as attractive to women as it is to men? Possibly not. There is no practical way to objectively determine whether Cool is as prevalent among women as men, but experience suggests that it is not – that although Cool is a strategy that women understand and can wield as well as men, fewer of them actually choose to do so. This goes to the heart of one of the continuing debates in feminism, namely whether women should be striving for absolute parity with men – to do all the things that men do – or whether, as Germaine Greer and others suggest, they should be going further, to develop aspects of female character that have so far been suppressed.

In thinking about Cool and women, at least four different hypotheses seem plausible: (1) that Cool has always been equally deployed by men and women, but that it doesn't work so well for women; (2) that Cool has always been, and always will be, a purely male stratagem, an important aim of which is to maximize personal freedom and sexual conquest while minimizing commitment; (3) that the Cool pose has always been equally usable by both young men and women, but that childbearing and rearing makes it difficult or undesirable for women to persist with it in later life (put more bluntly, women grow out of it whereas many men don't); (4) that Cool has historically been a predominantly male stratagem, but now increased personal freedom, affluence, education and the invention of effective contraception are making it evermore attractive to women.

It's hard to imagine what sorts of statistics or experiments could distinguish between these hypotheses, so all we can do is offer a guess, which is that the truth lies in some combination of 1, 3 and 4.

The first hypothesis, that Cool just doesn't work so well for women is plausible enough. Examination of the biographies of Cool women like Holiday or Joplin suggests that they were even more emotionally damaged by their 'on-the-edge' lifestyles than their male contemporaries. One might go on to argue that a male-dominated society punishes women who transgress harder than it does men, but that is just to say that the hypothesis is true, if Cool is a way of coping with society's disapproval that works for many men.

Hypotheses 1 and 3 both hint that biological factors might be at work, which will be anathema to some feminists, but must be considered. Modern contraceptive methods make it possible for women to choose when to have children, or not to have them at all, so they too could choose to adopt a Cool lifestyle of unbridled hedonism and sexual conquest. However, so fundamental a matter as the reproduction of a species is never likely to be that simple.

Recent developments in evolutionary psychology, well-summarized in Steven Pinker's *How the Mind Works* (1998), suggest that there is indeed a significant genetic component to human personality and that evolution has caused this component to differ between men and women, reflecting different interests in the struggle for reproductive success. To paraphrase the argument roughly, man's genetic interest is in availability and fertility so as to spread his genes more widely, while a woman's genetic interest is to find, and keep, the best-quality man she can whose fitness and resources will improve the survival chances of her children. Natal Angier in *Woman: An Intimate Geography* (1999) has suggested that this picture is too simple – without denying the validity of evolutionary explanations per se – and that alternative strategies are available for both sexes. For men 'mate guarding' – that is preventing other males from impregnating their mate – may be a more efficient strategy than promiscuity in many circumstances, and might account for the invention of the institution of marriage. Remarking that human fertility is low, taking on average 120 occasions of regular intercourse to get pregnant, Angier suggests that a man has a choice of two equally effective strategies:

he can sleep with a lot of women (the quantitative approach) or he can sleep with one woman for months at a time, and be madly in love with her (the qualitative approach). Recent research in animal biology also reveals the extent to which infidelity can be an important strategy for both sexes, as a woman might 'win' in evolutionary terms by catching a reliable and protective spouse but secretly getting pregnant by a more adventurous type who would make a terrible spouse (in our terms a Cool jerk).

Such theories do not amount to saying that human beings are robots totally controlled by their genes, nor are they incompatible with the existence of free will or morality. Genetic characteristics are only tendencies, not wholly determining, and they provide a material basis for the 'instincts' that religion, art, philosophy, and more recently psychoanalysis, have described for centuries, the motivations that underlie our expressed emotions. The way humans actually behave is always a complex interaction between learned rules, rational deliberation and these unconscious motives: Neo-Darwinists now believe, based on identical twin studies, that the relative contributions of 'nature' (genetic inheritance) and 'nurture' (social conditioning) to an individual's character is around 50:50.

So if there *are* real instinctual differences between men and women, they might not be wholly predictive for individuals but might be expected to produce different group behaviours. What this means for our argument is that to whatever extent nature does overcome nurture, women might be less attracted to a Cool strategy, that seeks to avoid deep emotional commitment, for psychological reasons that in turn stem from hormonal, that is biological, roots. This is quite over and above any social and economic issues such as child support, from which contraception *in theory* frees women. In short, the detachment so central to the Cool pose may not come as 'naturally' to women as it does to men, because they have evolved a hormonally mediated tendency to emotional attachment to assist bonding with their children. It's not hard to see why feminists would have to reject such a suggestion if it were posed in the form of a 'maternal instinct', but it is now widely accepted in more diffuse terms, for example in claims that women are more 'emotionally literate' than men.

The related question, as to why Cool succeeds as a male strategy – that is, why women so often fall for Cool jerks who ultimately mistreat them – provides a never-ending source of subject matter for popular drama. Evolutionary psychology must say that if women are genetically predisposed to seek fitness in their mates, then conspicuous sexual success (which is the goal of any Cool man) can be taken as evidence that the successful man is considered 'fit' by their peers, like the peacock with the biggest tail.

We will be suggesting later that Cool serves as a defence against depression induced by subjugation, embarrassment and competition, and in particular by the threat to self-esteem posed by 'maladaptive comparison' with perfect media stereotypes. The continual rise in eating disorders suggests that maladaptive comparison may disproportionately affect young women, and indeed it appears that women are roughly twice as likely to be depressed as men in most Western societies. The reasons for this disparity are complex and not yet fully understood, although Catherine Hakim's researches into the conflicting pressures of work and family on women are illuminating. It might be plausible therefore to suggest that Cool is a less effective defensive strategy for women than it is for men, either because they don't employ it, or because it doesn't work so well when they do.

If there is anything to the hypothesis that women are biologically or psychologically less attracted to Cool, that would suggest two possible paths of development: effective contraception and the social effects of feminism might prompt more women to overcome their reluctance and start acting Cool, on the other hand, many women might examine the implications of Cool and decide that they want no part of it, that they need to invent an alternative strategy that fits the female psyche better. Both these developments are actually occurring all around us: the phenomenon of 'girl power' is just one sign that many school-age girls in the late '90s aspire to be as Cool as the lads, while the twin phenomena of 'political correctness' and the 'therapy movement' could be seen as female-friendly alternatives to Cool. Both developments sprang from the '60s counter-culture, but have been transformed by the influence of radical feminism, and gay and anti-racist activism. Both rejected the macho-sexual hedonism of Cool, but share some of its other transgressive and libertarian beliefs. Both part company from Cool in insisting on unfettered emotional expression in place of ironic detachment, which could very well be seen as a feminization of Cool.

Gay Cool

One reason why the Cool male appeals to women is that behind his dangerous and rebellious front there lurks an interest in personal appearance and bearing that is closer to feminine attitudes than to the average straight male's utilitarian non-style. This interest is also closer to the attitude of many male homosexuals, and the influence of gay culture on the development of Cool is something that deserves much closer study. Historically it is indisputable that many of the original Cool screen icons, such as James Dean and Steve McQueen, were either gay or bi-sexual, and those who were not, like Paul Newman and Robert Redford, were as powerfully attractive to gay men as to women. The pivotal role that gay males played in the beat movement is equally indisputable, given that Allen Ginsberg and William Burroughs were both gay, while Jack Kerouac and Neal Cassady were bisexual.

We hinted in an earlier chapter that centuries of persecution of

Paul Newman and Elizabeth Taylor in Richard Brooks's 1958 film *Cat on a Hot Tin Roof*: Cool cat meets hot tin. Most of Newman's best work is powered by a similar emotional temperature gradient . . .

homosexuals might have created the need for a defensive psychic strategy very similar to Cool. In Susan Sontag's seminal 1964 essay on Camp sensibility, she identifies many aspects of Camp that are remarkably similar to our conception of Cool, such as its hedonism, love of irony, exaggeration and 'bad taste' and the reluctance to be judgmental. Nevertheless, it would be rash to try to assimilate Camp and Cool as exactly the same sensibility, because traditionally High Camp is considered to be lighter and more frivolous than Cool. In his obituary of Noel Coward, the seminal British critic Kenneth Tynan observed this same connection:

> Coward invented the concept of cool, and may have had emotional reasons for doing so. At all events, he made camp elegant, and wore a mask of amused indifference – 'Grin and

rise above it' – to disguise any emotions he preferred not to reveal. From the beginning of his career he was a shrugger-off of passion and a master of understatement . . . [4]

That said, the development of gay culture over recent decades has seen a darkening of gay sensibilities, from the coke-and-poppers orgies of '70s San Francisco and New York disco and bath-house scenes, through the trauma of the AIDS epidemic, to the current vogue for sado-masochism and fetishism. As Sontag had already spotted, a certain gay sensibility was at work in the aesthetics of Warhol's brand of Pop Art which she characterized as 'more flat and more dry, more serious, more detached, ultimately nihilistic' than previous manifestations.[5]

However, the fact that gays are attracted to Cool doesn't necessarily mean that Cool is always fond of gays. One of the more notable features of Cool in most of its manifestations is tolerance, letting other people 'do their own thing', be what they want to be and express themselves as they wish. An exception to this rule of tolerance would appear to be the latent (or not so latent) misogyny and homophobia that lurks within some strains of Cool; convincing evidence that it originated as a male, heterosexual strategy. For example, it is no coincidence that those cartoon anti-heroes Beavis and Butthead classify everything they encounter as either 'Cool' or else 'It sucks' – the underlying semantics of which suggest that performing fellatio is so contemptible that it has become the strongest possible term of abuse (although being on the receiving end is highly desirable). For instance the President of the USA, the most powerful man in the world, doesn't suck, he gets sucked. The virulent homophobia of current black musical forms – most particularly gangsta rap and dance hall reggae which boast about shooting 'faggots' and 'batty bwoys' – appears to play a significant part in its attraction for teenage white males. This is not an especially new phenomenon as teenage boys have always sought reassurance against any sexual ambivalence they might be feeling through aggressively macho behaviour.

Male homosexuality is an even stronger taboo in most African cultures than it is in white societies, and perhaps this taboo has been transmitted into modern Cool. Certainly the homophobic and misogynistic elements seem to be growing stronger in gangsta rap, which fits in well with a worship of guns, violence and money but offers a stark contrast to the sensibility expressed in, for example, the lyrics of Marvin Gaye's *Sexual Healing* or the 'lurve' schmaltz of Barry White. Could it perhaps be that the motivation is actually just to shock the sensibilities of politically correct white liberals? If so it is extremely effective, and one might be tempted to understand rap lyrics as a historical extension of the 'Dirty Dozens', that is, a sort of game for testing the strength of your opponent's Cool. Whether or not this is the motive, black Cool is certainty going through a hyper-macho phase of which homophobia is but one aspect.

CHAPTER EIGHT

Cool Psyche

There is, then, a familiar type of composure that creates an
appearance of self-possession . . . The mind creates a distance
in the self – often in the form of an irony – from its own desire,
from the affective core of the self, and manages, by the same
token, a distance from everybody else. A sometimes compelling
but ambiguous aura, by communicating a relative absence of
neediness, renders the other dispensable. And this is done
partly through projection; at its most extreme, the neediness
is evoked in the people around and then treated with sadistic
dismay, as though it were an obnoxious stranger. Hell is not
other people but one's need for other people.

Adam Phillips[1]

Since the '50s large numbers of relatively affluent white people have
adopted the Cool attitude, and that raises the question of whether theirs
was purely an aesthetic decision, or whether there is some deeper psychological explanation; after all, if the origins of Cool lie in the experience
of oppression, it is not immediately obvious why it should be attractive

to those who are comfortable. To answer this question we should start by looking at what psychological role Cool plays among those African-Americans who first elaborated it.

In the days of slavery Cool was part of a 'survival mentality', a defence mechanism invented to cope with continuous exploitation, discrimination and disadvantage: it deployed ironic detachment and emotional impassivity to enable its bearer to withstand the domineering orders, abuse and insults of the overseer without succumbing either to depression or to a rage that might incur flogging or even execution.

In *Cool Pose* (1992) Richard Majors and Janet Mancini Billson investigated the psychological function of Cool among urban black-American youth of the '90s, and concluded that:

> For some black males, cool pose represents a fundamental structuring of the psyche – the cool mask belies the rage held in check beneath the surface. For others it is the adoption of a uniquely creative style that serves as a sign of belonging and stature. Black males have learned to use posing and posturing to communicate power, toughness, detachment, and style-self. They have developed a 'third eye' that reads interpersonal situations with a special acuity. They have cultivated a keen sense of what to say, and how and when to say it, in order to avoid punishment and pain, and to embellish their life chances.[2]

So according to Majors and Mancini Billson, Cool has two distinct but interlocking functions, one negative (to suppress rage), and one positive (to express group identity through personal style).

As a survival strategy Cool is not an unqualified success. Keeping his Cool might keep a black youth out of trouble on the streets, but that same attitude may be misinterpreted by teachers and employers as being 'lazy', 'slow' or 'insolent' and therefore become the cause of exclusion from school or loss of a job. The authors identify black Cool, at least in the early '90s, as a predominantly, although not entirely, male phenomenon and one which may have a tragically negative effect on personal relationships by inhibiting the development of real intimacy with partners. They accept Robert Farris Thompson's ideas concerning the West African origins of Cool and trace its evolution into the well-documented 'masking' behaviour of American black men – a kind of acting and role-playing used as a defensive strategy. They argue for a broad definition of Cool that encompasses psychological stances, body language, verbal styles like shucking, joking and inversion (i.e. irony) and an aesthetic that they call 'expressive styling', which describes the flamboyant behaviours and dress-codes of everyone from sports personalities and musicians to pimps, hustlers and gangstas.

Two of Majors and Mancini Billson's observations are of particular relevance to our question. They insist that flamboyance and exuberance can be just another aspect of Cool – thereby ruling out narrow definitions of Cool rooted solely in its 'tasteful' '50s manifestations – and they make a crucial connection between the childhood game called 'the dozens', which involves making obscene insults against your opponents' family (of which the ubiquitous 'motherfucker' is but a mild example) and the violent and misogynistic trends displayed in rap and hip-hop lyrics. Playing 'the dozens' may be likened to a commando training-course in Cool, which teaches children how to cope with verbal abuse without cracking.

Relative Deprivation

So why would affluent, middle-class white people come to adopt such a defence mechanism? The answer lies in profound changes to the socialization process that have taken place in Western countries as a consequence of affluence. In particular, commentators have noted how the insecurity of poverty is being replaced by other causes of anxiety, stress and depression. These include the loss of supportive relationships brought about by increased individualism and personal autonomy, decreasing job security, changes in family structures and child-rearing habits, increased competition and the phenomenon of 'relative deprivation' (a sociologized version of 'plain old envy') wherein people judge their state of well-being relative to those better off than themselves, rather than in absolute terms.

Post-war affluence and social levelling offered parents from the '50s onwards opportunities for personal autonomy undreamt of by the pre-war generations, but as a consequence they became less willing wholly to subordinate their lives to child rearing, the 'fate' that was accepted as natural and inevitable by previous generations (excepting the aristocracy and the very rich). This new affluence changed child-rearing habits permanently, producing a relaxation of the older strict disciplines, and a lavishing of material benefits, combined with a shallower emotional relationship to the children because parents now placed a higher priority on their own right to self-fulfillment.

In *The Culture of Narcissism* (1979) the late Christopher Lasch claimed to identify a new personality type which he called the 'liberated personality' among patients who were presenting themselves for psychotherapy in the '70s. This new personality was, according to Lasch, characterized by manipulative charm, pseudo-awareness of one's condition, promiscuous pan-sexuality, fascination with oral sex, hypochondria, protective emotional shallowness, avoidance of dependence, inability to mourn, and dread of old age and death: a catalogue which touches, in many respects, on our concept of the Cool personality. For Lasch these character traits stemmed from childhood fantasies of exaggerated personal beauty and omnipotence, created to fend off an impotent rage induced by feelings of abandonment or neglect, which Lasch attributed to the new liberal child-rearing practices of the '50s and '60s. Cool parents rear Cool children by spoiling them materially while offering only relatively shallow emotional guidance.

Suppressed rage at absent or distant parents might explain why Cool is so profoundly anti-family: your parents are almost by definition Uncool, and you can only construct a Cool persona for yourself outside of the intrusions and responsibilities of family life. An example of anti-family feeling is often observable among homeless young people who report that they 'only feel in control on the street'. In the mind of teenage runaways the city street, even with all its terrible deprivations, becomes 'a cool place' where they can (among a community of peers and bolstered by drugs) feel in control. It is actually preferred to a home life where they were seen as disruptive and unwanted cuckoos in the nest, or to the childrens' home or similar institution with abusive intrusions of its own.

The position of parents has been weakened further still by having to compete with the enormous expansion of the mass media – particularly

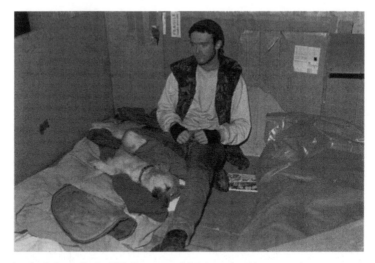

London's South Bank, 1989. For many of the young homeless, even the deprivations of life on the street are preferable to a family life in which they did not feel in control.

television cartoons, commercials and life style magazines – for influence over their child's imagination. Social psychologists have long studied the ways in which people maintain self esteem: by comparing themselves socially against their peers, ranking their peers and situating themselves within that ranking, they maintain an equilibrium by discounting the fact that some are better off than themselves against the fact that others are worse off. However, our ever more intrusive mass media and the cult of celebrity they promote threaten to disrupt this delicate mechanism. We are faced every day with images of the richest, most beautiful and most fulfilled people on the planet and compared to them, everyone feels like a loser.

The British psychologist Oliver James in *Britain On the Couch* (1998) has called this effect 'maladaptive social comparison', building on a long-standing theoretical tradition in sociology that stems from the ideas of Thomas Merton. This holds that in conditions of affluence our aspirations are socially contrived to always overshoot reality. James blames such comparison, at least in part, for the inexorable rise in the incidence of clinical depression which threatens to become the leading cause of mental illness in Western societies. One American survey, cited by James, followed 18,000 people and showed that those born between 1945 and 1955 were three to ten times more likely to be diagnosed as clinically depressed before the age of 34 than those born between 1904 and 1914. James argues that people who succumb to depression do so because they compare themselves to unrealistically-high celebrity-set norms in a destructive way, while healthy people find ways of comparison which play up their own qualities and discount the advantages that celebrities possess.

We would hypothesize further (although James himself does not touch on the subject) that Cool is precisely one such mechanism that people use to short-circuit maladaptive comparisons and avoid depression. Sociological theories such as 'strain' theory support the idea that school students who feel that they are failing in the classroom, or who do not 'fit in' socially, adopt a strategy of disengagement from school activities, and develop anti-academic cliques, or subcultures, that provide an alternative route to self-esteem. By acting Cool you declare yourself to be a non-participant in the bigger race, for if you don't share 'straight' society's values then you can stop comparing yourself to them. Cool cannot abolish social comparisons entirely, but it can restrict their scope to your immediate peer group. Mods, rockers, skinheads, punks, hippies, crusties, goths: for several successive generations of marginalized and disaffected young people these subcultures, with their own rules, rituals and obligations, have provided a *magical* alternative to being written off as a hopeless loser in the rat race. In the language of youth subcultures, 'I'm cool' equates to 'I'm in control.'

The psychological essence of Cool is self-invention, coupled to a hyper-acute awareness of such self-invention in other people; it amounts to the creation of a calm psychic mask to hide inner disturbance. A 1977 oil by American artist Alex Katz.

So what Cool has offered to groups as disparate as field slaves, jazz musicians, disillusioned war veterans, Detroit street gangs, teenage runaways and middle-class high school dissenters is a kind of mental empowerment that their circumstances otherwise fail to supply. In this sense Cool is a subcultural alternative to the old notion of personal dignity, since dignity – that which Adorno called 'the supreme bourgeois concept' – is a quality that is validated by the established institutions of church, state and work. Cool, on the other hand, is a form of self-worth that is validated primarily by the way your personality, appearance and attitude are adjudged by your own peers. Nevertheless, the association between Cool, addiction and suicide suggests that as a *real* solution to living in a highly competitive society, it is only partially effective. Studies continue to show that the academic performance of many boys deteriorates rapidly between thirteen and nineteen as they come to see learning and academic success as 'girlish' and 'uncool', and this disabling tendency among boys is being accompanied by increases in the rate of suicide and attempted suicide.

I'm Hip to That

Cool detachment if pursued to its limit would lead to sociopathy and total isolation, but there is within it a countervailing tendency that unites close peer groups through a shared idea about what 'cool' means – precisely those self-invented codes of dress, hairstyle, ritual, attitude and slang that Majors and Mancini Billson call 'expressive styling'. But it is also this very tendency that opens the loophole through which the advertising industry has colonized Cool and used it to sell goods to the young (and not-so-young).

Cool's mechanism of social cohesion, the counterbalance to its distancing effect, involves sharing knowledge of some secret that is denied to members of respectable or mainstream society. This was the original meaning of that synonym for Cool, 'hip', which was used as in 'I'm hip to that.' The content of this shared secret may be many different things, from the appreciation of a certain style of music, to predilection for a particular illegal drug, participation in crime, or some forbidden sexual practice. However, in the background there is always the hint of a bigger, seldom-verbalized, more abstract secret, namely the perceived hypocrisy of 'straight' society. Cool people share a belief that society's taboos have no moral force for them, and that these taboos are in any case regularly broken by even its most supposedly respectable members.

This big secret has many facets which encompass all the most important aspects of existence. Sex: even the President of the USA, even your preacher, even your parents do it. Family: 'They fuck you up, your mum and dad.' Money: everyone has their price, they'll all try to rip

Hip originally meant sharing some secret that was denied to 'squares' – the appreciation of a certain style of music, a liking for a particular illegal drug or some forbidden sexual practice.

you off. Politics: the good guys never win, all politicians are liars. Crime: the only real crime is getting caught. Drugs: they tell us drugs are nasty, but drugs feel good, so 'they' are either liars or hypocrites. Death: we're all going to die, so what's the use of worrying. This quality of worldly knowingness is absolutely central to the Cool personality, which always wants to know everything and loathes secrecy, concealment and duplicity. In essence then the psychological core of Cool is self-invention coupled to a hyper-acute awareness of such self-invention by other people. It amounts to the creation of a calm psychic mask to hide inner disturbance, whether rage at racist mistreatment, anxiety in the face of competition or merely a furious urge for sexual conquest. It's no coincidence that Cool became the dominant attitude in a Hollywood where self-invention is a way of life, and this supplies us with a plausible mechanism for the reproduction and dissemination of Cool. Celebrities invent an unattainably attractive Cool personality, an image which makes insecure teenage fans feel so inadequate that adopting the Cool pose is in turn *their* only way of coping with their enhanced anxiety. Repeat ad infinitum.

The self-invented nature of Cool also explains its profound distrust of authority, which can often amount to a unilateral declaration of independence from social responsibility. All society's major institutions: government, the courts, the police, schools, hospitals etc. – require that their agents be accorded a degree of professional dignity in order to function. This involves a certain 'suspension of disbelief'. You know, for example, that a high-court judge is a human being like yourself, who eats, sleeps, excretes and copulates, but that knowledge is to be put aside when you stand before the court. The Cool persona refuses to suspend disbelief, seeing authority figures as just mask-wearers like itself, and the result is a loss of respect for authority figures that has been a notable feature of most democratic societies over the past decade (and is the source of much disquiet among social conservatives). As an example, one could cite the weakening of deference toward the royal family and House of Lords in the UK.

This inability to suspend disbelief along with an insistence on uncovering all of the world's sins also constitute Cool's Achilles heel as a strategy. Anxiety may be deflected by refusing to play the game, but insisting on uncovering all the most gruesome aspects of reality merely breeds new anxieties – which are often more virulent and less rooted in the everyday, and hence less tractable. The results can be frankly pathological, and this is where we should look for explanations of the love affair between Cool and violence, which reaches its creepy consummation in high-school massacres and flirtations with satanism and neo-Nazism. On the other hand it is possible to relearn how to suspend disbelief, to eschew irony and repudiate hedonism, hence the world-wide resurgence of religious and political fundamentalisms which offer various forms of faith, in place of detachment, as the required psychic shield. From the Islamic Taliban to the Christian 'right to life' movements, these are the sworn enemies of Cool.

The Touchy-feely Tendency

It would be difficult to say anything about the psychology of Cool without at least attempting to deal with a contemporary phenomenon which might appear to be its exact opposite: we refer of course to that heightened emotionalism for which there is as yet no adequate name, but is described by phrases such as the 'confessional culture', 'therapy culture', or more derogatorily as 'psychobabble' or the 'touchy-feely' tendency. This is the world of tabloid and celebrity television and journalism, of *Ally McBeal*, *Oprah* and *The Jerry Springer Show*, and of the mass-grieving following the death of Princess Diana. The single most important characteristic of this phenomenon is its belief that the free expression of

A return to an earlier state of affairs when people had greater emotional engagement with their peers? Emotional history seen as an ocean whose tide was ebbing but has now turned? We think not.

emotions is essential to mental health, fostered especially in the USA by more than half a century of exposure to many forms of psychotherapy. Another characteristic is frequently the conviction that one's self-hood has been damaged by past emotional traumas and repression, and a consequent desire to confess or reveal such events, which has lead to an alternative description as the 'victim culture'.

For our argument the important question this phenomenon raises is simply: does it contradict what we are saying about the growing influence of Cool? It is tempting to accept the 'therapy culture' at its face value, as evidence of a shift backwards to an earlier state of affairs in which people had greater emotional engagement with their peers, a model, if you like, of emotional history as an ocean whose tide was ebbing but has now turned. We do not believe this to be the case, and propose that on the contrary this 'therapy culture' springs from some of the same roots as Cool, and forms part of its development rather than any return to a previous condition. There are several possible grounds for thinking this. Having just argued that Cool operates as a defence mechanism against the depression and anxiety induced by a highly competitive society, we have also admitted that it is a very imperfect defence and that furthermore, maintaining Cool actually imposes its own different kind of psychic strain. It is significant that Christopher Lasch first detected his 'narcis-sistic persona' among patients who had sought therapy for feelings of emptiness and 'vague, diffuse feelings of dissatisfaction with life'. Cool and therapy can not only co-exist but may even feed on one another (in those strata of society that can afford therapy, that is) as tabloid exposures of the lives of celebrities so often reveal. The detached and reckless hell-raiser who spends the weekends with his shrink has become a cliché among Hollywood actors, rock stars, country singers, and business high-flyers.

To make this coexistence more uneasy still, certain strands in popular culture are currently promoting nostalgia for a pre-Cool paradise, a world ruled by real passion and untrammelled emotion. We refer of course to the work of certain best-selling film directors, in particular James Cameron and Steven Spielberg. The plots of Cameron's *Titanic* and Spielberg's *Saving Private Ryan* both employ the same formula of starting in the present day with a bunch of Cool kids meeting up with a survivor from a 'golden age' of sentiment and undergoing a 'learning experience' as a result. (A similar device may be seen at work in the plot of the 1999 low-budget hit movie *The Blair Witch Project*.) The fact that this formula works so well suggests that there is a widespread anxiety about what has been lost in the pursuit of Cool, but it does *not* demonstrate that a majority of young people really want (or could tolerate) a return to the conditions of material deprivation and sexual repression that spawned the romanticism and self-sacrifice these films so enticingly depict.

However, there are deeper connections still between Cool and the 'therapy culture', namely that all this suffering and victimhood has a suspiciously competitive undertone to it. To discover that one is a 'victim' is to make oneself special, to remove oneself from the ranks of the ordinary, and that is also the prime motivation of Cool. In a perceptive article in the *New York Review of Books* Ian Buruma made the case that victimhood is the moving spirit of our times (in effect occupying the position that we attribute to Cool) where growing numbers of people want to feel themselves part of some oppressed minority: in effect they are demanding an equal share of the historical pain of the Holocaust and other great historical tragedies. The vehicle for this pursuit of psychic-integrity-through-suffering is what Buruma caustically describes as a 'vulgar Freudianism' which all too easily collapses into kitsch sentimentality of the Oprah Winfrey or Jerry Springer kind. Memory, whether of the great historical injustices or of our own childhood mis-treatment, becomes elevated to the status of unquestionable testimony.

In Buruma's words '. . . enlightenment is probably not the issue here. Instead there is authenticity. When all truth is subjective, only feelings are authentic, and only the subject can know whether his or her feelings are true or false.'[3] This observation fits well with our view of a Cool which equally seeks the authentic, in order to set itself apart from the inauthentic. A particular form that authenticity can take is intensity of feeling or suffering: in effect one is saying, 'I feel more intensely than you, I have suffered more than you, you are all smug, complacent nobodies.'

We observed earlier that many of the 'disciplines' of the therapy movement actually emerged from various strands within the '60s counter-culture. Hence, these 'disciplines' also share historical roots with our notion of Cool, to the point where one is tempted to wonder if the therapeutic attitude is not just a different kind of Cool mask, one that pretends to care a lot. The real difference lies not perhaps in the emotional temperature, but in the fact that this sentimentalizing tendency lacks all trace of the irony that we see as being an essential component of Cool.

CHAPTER NINE

Cool Rules

The fact that the term [Cool] has maintained standard popularity among youth into the '90s may plausibly suggest not only the culture's ongoing potency but also the continued elaboration of its results.

Peter N. Stearns[1]

What you've got to understand is that 14 to 16-year-olds will always dictate what's cool and what's not. We dictate what's gonna go on in fashion, music and everything. We're conquering the world.

Will Nicholls, aged 14, 'coolest kid around'[2]

In a 1998 article for *The New York Review of Books* Mark Lilla of the Princeton University Institute of Advanced Studies pondered the two revolutions that have transformed post-war America – the 'cultural' revolution of the '60s and Reagan's neo-liberal economic revolution of the '80s – and was very critical of the inadequate political responses to their aftermath from both the right and the left of American politics. He characterizes their responses as 'reactionary' in the proper usage of the term: that is, the right can only react by lambasting the moral laxity bequeathed by the '60s, while the left reacts by railing helplessly against the triumph of Reaganomics. The facts are, as Lilla puts it, that 'the Sixties happened, Reagan happened and for the foreseeable future they will together define our political horizon'. According to Lilla, young Americans have no difficulty in reconciling the two in their daily lives, 'holding down day jobs in the unfettered global economy while spending weekends immersed in a moral and cultural universe shaped by the Sixties'.[3]

These thoughts then prompted Lilla to pose a dramatic question 'for which neither de Tocqueville, nor Marx, nor Weber had prepared us: what principle in the American creed has simultaneously made possible these seemingly contradictory revolutions? How have our notions of equality and individualism been transformed to support a morally lax yet economically successful capitalist society?'[4] At the risk of some immodesty towards the shades of de Tocqueville, Marx and Weber we offer a single-word answer to Lilla: Cool.

Far from being a mere matter of fashionable slang, sartorial style, or some passing behavioural fad, Cool provides that psychological structure through which the longest-standing contradiction in Western societies – that between the necessity for work and the desirability of play – is apparently being resolved. In short, Cool appears to be usurping the work ethic itself, to become installed as the dominant mindset of advanced consumer capitalism. According to Peter Stearns, 'With new emotional criteria for work as a fulcrum, American society has been engaged in a significant effort to change the rules of emotionality – an effort not always explicit and often masked by injunctions of emotional permissiveness designed in fact to increase controls.'[5]

The low levels of unionization and the increasing rarity of either organized industrial action or unofficial workplace-based protest testify to the effectiveness of an emotional style more appropriate to the demands of working in a deregulated economy. By making a decisive break with the work ethic, Cool can cover all the angles. For those in well-paid jobs, the workplace itself can become Cool, with casual dress and little perks like an espresso machine and being on first-name terms with your boss. There may be no pension benefits, but the financial-services sector is queuing up to handle that for you with a smile. As for those with no jobs, well of course Cool (liberally assisted by drugs) has always been the refuge of the underdog – that is after all where it came from.

'This book, being about work, is, by its very nature, about violence – to the spirit as well as to the body.'[6] So began Studs Terkel's classic critique of modern labour relations. Terkel's message was a traditional Marxist one, namely that no-one will employ you unless they can make a profit out of you, and hence that capitalism inevitably creates wage-slavery, both in the office and on the factory floor. That harsh message is now replaced by the emollient notion of Cool work. Take a look around your local bookshop and it's likely you'll find that the business section boasts more hip-sounding titles than the politics or culture sections (for example: *First, Break All the Rules*; *1,001 Perfectly Legal Ways to Get Exactly What You Want, When You Want It, Every Time*) with upbeat messages of radical social change. This new benevolent face of capitalism is a direct consequence of Lilla's 'moral and cultural universe of the sixties'.

The counter-culture proved to be an excellent breeding ground for entrepreneurs: Jann Wenner, Richard Branson, Steve Jobs, Bill Gates, Felix Dennis, all created successful businesses in the burgeoning media, information technology and culture industries whose internal organization and ethos reflected counter-culture values. Ben & Jerry and Anita Roddick did the same in the food and cosmetics sectors, and there are many more examples. This notion that the workplace could be Cool may have originated among a counter-cultural minority, but it has spread to affect many previously 'straight' firms as new young management take over from the Second World War generation. Hip entrepreneurs like

'60s counterculture proved to be an excellent breeding ground for entrepreneurs, including Steve Jobs, Ben and Jerry, and Felix Dennis, shown here.

Branson and Gates retain a belief that they are engaged in socially subversive projects, that they are in some sense 'anti-establishment', even after their businesses have become huge and highly profitable. Their success has helped transform mainstream business culture to the extent that, as Thomas Frank puts it 'What happened in the sixties is that hip (or cool) became central to the way capitalism understood itself and explained itself to the public.'[7]

This 'Cool workplace' message is rapidly usurping traditional critiques of work relations such as Terkel's. In the Cool workplace notions like 'us and them' and 'jobs for life' disappear, as does the notion that workers will have long-standing loyalties to a particular company. Richard Sennet's *The Corrosion of Character* (New York, 1998) shows how the new enterprise now demands not loyalty but flexibility without which the modern employee is deemed unable to cope with increasing organizational complexity. Significantly, such ideas are not being pushed by the conservative right but by centrist social democratic parties such as Clinton's Democrats and Blair's New Labourites. One could argue that the

Cool mindset underlies Tony Blair's promotion of a 'third way' for social democracy in the twenty-first century – a way in which employees and managers act in partnership for the greater good (even if they sometimes overlook rather Uncool disparities in the distribution of the rewards).

The work of sociologist Anthony Giddens is seen by many people as providing the intellectual underpinning for New Labour policies and although Giddens makes no reference to Cool, he deploys a clearly related concept of 'reflexive modernization' by which he means that people are becoming more responsible for steering their own lives and less dependent on outside institutions. As he puts it, 'My relationship to modern society – my social identity – has become unglued from the contexts, communities and expectations that once circumscribed my (and your) knowledge of who I am and how I live. Today I am responsible and liable for my own identity.'[8] That sounds very much like a description of the positive aspect of Cool detachment. Giddens stresses that this new democratized, flexible form of capitalism creates uncertainty, and that the public welfare services must be reconstructed to act as a buffer if widespread discontent is to be avoided. However, it is by no means certain that employers, who love the flexibility element, are so keen on this side of the equation. Flexibility can mean insecurity and de-skilling, accelerated by the abandonment of unions and collective bargaining as the means to promote the interests of employees.

Doonesbury Flashbacks

BY GARRY TRUDEAU

It is likely that the Cool workplace will be effective in defusing any renaissance of labour militancy and trade-union organization, which mirrors the disappearance of state socialist solutions from the political arena. It might prove more productive for employees instead to take the notion of the Cool workplace to its logical conclusion, by campaigning strongly for employee share schemes, so that what at the moment is a largely cosmetic transformation might progress to a more genuine commonality of interests grounded in economics.

Competitive Consumption

College kids, gently unkempt. They stood between the shelves talking and browsing, going through the product boxes, and others mixed in, slightly older men and women, they had professions and soft slacks and knife pleats and a certain ease of bearing and belonging, the package of attitudes and values known as lifestyle.[9]

It is no coincidence that we have described Cool as almost the antithesis of the Christian virtues of faith, hope, and charity. Nor does Cool have much in common with the more specifically Protestant virtues of hard work, thrift and self-discipline – or for that matter the secular virtues of old-time Labourism which one might characterize as compassion, modesty and temperance. Advanced capitalism no longer depends on such sober and puritanical notions of virtue to maintain its labour discipline. Cool is a new mode of individualism, flexible enough to cope with the pace of transformation of work in the deregulated global economy. It is far better adapted to a life of service and consumption than one of toil and sacrifice. It is this that provides the missing 'cement' to fill that contradiction implied in Mark Lilla's question. In other words, Cool enables people to live with uncertainty and lowered expectations, by concentrating on present pleasures. In short, when the going gets tough, the Cool go shopping.

Cool as an ethic is exquisitely suited to a life of consumption rather than production because the competitive spirit that we see hiding beneath the detached surface presented by Cool can drive new, adventurous and more discriminating modes of consumption, while simultaneously offering a handle by which Cool advertisers can steer the consumer in the desired direction. To characterize the way this new Cool consumer individualism operates, perhaps we could be forgiven for coining a new phrase: the 'competitive consumption of experience'. Everyone is a rebel now, no-one is ordinary, no-one wants to be a face in the crowd, everyone wants intense experiences: indeed everyone wants *more* intense experiences than their friends and neighbours. People have a mental checklist of intense experiences that need to be collected: climb the mountain; watch a volcano erupt; swim with the dolphins; have multiple orgasms . . . The media understand this greed for the superlative, and their hyperbolic coverage of each newly fashionable leisure activity veers toward the condition of pornography, giving us food-porn, travel-porn, garden-porn, car-porn, and decor-porn.

Radical critics of consumerism, from Marcuse to Debord, have always proceeded from the observation that capitalism manufactures false needs and implants them in the passive populace via advertising, consumption being seen as a chore that must be imposed to keep the wheels of production turning and the surplus value flowing. For example, in *The Society of the Spectacle* Debord employed the concept of 'pseudo-needs', as in this formulation:

> It is doubtless impossible to contrast the pseudo-need imposed by the reign of modern consumerism with any authentic need or desire that is not in itself equally determined by society and its history. But the commodity in the stage of its abundance

attests to an absolute break in the organic development of social needs.[10]

Unfortunately anyone who tries to wield such arguments within practical politics invariably ends up by attempting that 'impossible contrast' and arguing that some social needs are more authentic than others, which in turn raises the deadly question of who will be the judge of such authenticity. Very soon one finds oneself back on the terrain of that terrible old joke whose punch-line is: 'after the revolution you will eat strawberry ice-cream, *and like it!*' By embracing popular culture and loosening up the workplace, Cool businesses can ever more quickly determine what consumers want and adapt and innovate to 'satisfy' them, while the Cool consumers are increasingly in charge of their own consumption and so no coercion is required (unless of course one tries to avoid paying the bill).

Cool has moved from being the pose of a tiny minority and is fast becoming the majority attitude among young people. Far from being a passing fad it is having a major effect on business and even on our political life. Although Cool is deployed by the culture industries and international media conglomerates as 'an aesthetic for the exercise of economic power', that doesn't mean that they invented Cool as an instrument of oppression: on the contrary they find it among the customers themselves, and then only with some difficulty. The price of Cool is eternal vigilance, and advertisers with a young audience play a difficult game, forced constantly to update their campaigns and demonstrate their knowledge about new people, new looks and new music: a whole new profession has arisen, the 'youth consultant' who travels around the country (on expenses) watching the clubs and the streets to discover what is Cool this month. Far from creating Cool, 'TV produces programmes and images for teens that reinforce already forged models of coolness'.[11]

Advertising is, according to Eric Hobsbawm, the symptom and the symbol par excellence of living in the material world, and increasingly that world is a Cool, ironic one. The levels of irony and self-reference in current, youth-oriented commercials grant them an irresistible and irrefutable circularity: if you don't like them or understand them, that can only be because you don't 'get' them, because you're not Cool enough. Such is the sophistication of the advertisers' reading of Cool that they are now capable of playing games with it, a highly successful example being the *faux naif* campaign for the orange-free drink Sunny Delight in which deliberate naffness is now identified by overly-knowing consumers as wholesome and healthy.

Cool elevates personal taste into a complete ethos in which you are what you like, and what you therefore buy, and it's accessible to any kid who can afford the correct brand of trainers (or if not, who can steal them) without requiring any tiresome study or practice. An endless range of advertised products, from cars and computers to mobile phones,

The levels of irony and self-reference in current youth-oriented commercials grant them an irresistible and irrefutable circularity: if you don't like them, it can only be because you don't 'get' them, because you're not Cool enough. A 1994 poster.

promise to alter young people's external appearance and hence change their internal mood. Cool is the liberated way to consume: it implies a critical awareness of the purpose of advertising, the knowledge that 'most of what they are trying to sell me is garbage, but I'm Cool, I know the difference'. Throughout the '90s these Cool values have been disseminated throughout the public language of advertising every bit as vigorously as a hundred years earlier the work ethic was preached to the workers from church pulpits.

Advertisers perhaps do not actually *construct* consumer subjectivity as some radical critics would have it, but they devote enormous effort to *discovering* and *reflecting* consumer subjectivity. The vendors of films, music, soft drinks, snack foods and sports wear – the life-staples of the young – have learned to be Cool and to use Cool. Advertising portrays a constantly updated collage of personal styles, postures and entertainments designed both to reflect and affect the way people think and feel about themselves and their society, and this is not merely a cynical manoeuvre perpetrated by manipulative outsiders whose real interests lie elsewhere. Most of the senior executive positions in our mass-media, marketing and advertising industries are now occupied by that generation that came of age in the late '60s, and this mediocracy knows how to deploy Cool as a selling tool, how to manipulate its icons, precisely because it makes sense to them, it reflects their own values. Marx's axiom that in every age the ruling ideas are the ideas of the ruling class is no less true because the economics did not go quite as planned. Cool has become the dominant ideology of the media professionals. Movie directors and script writers, television executives, record-company chiefs, magazine editors, computer-game designers and advertising creatives all share with their potential audience a taste for cynicism, sensuality, self-obsession, social indifference and ironic cruelty.

Surprisingly this personal adherence to Cool does not prevent the new mediocracy from addressing those sections of the paying audience –

the middle-aged and elderly in particular – who do not aspire, or even understand what it is to be Cool, and who prefer the old culture of sentimentality and easy emotion. A Cool producer can 'do' sentimental too, although probably with an ironic tongue in the cheek. Increasingly, touches of Cool irony are creeping into the most unashamedly populist of entertainments: a transvestite presenter here, a gay compère there. Peter Weir's 1998 movie *The Truman Show* brilliantly parodied the self-importance of this breed of Cool dream merchant, in the central role of Christof, played by Ed Harris, the beret-wearing Cool producer-deity. What could be cooler than having the power to 'cue the sun'? Crucially, the film does not portray Christof as a phoney or cynic, but as a zealot convinced of his Christ-like mission to inject emotion into the ordinariness of people's lives. The subtext is that Christof himself lacks the very emotion that he dispenses, a Cool ruler indeed. Just as the official ideology of communism was concerned to suppress all other possible versions of socialism, so the modern version of Cool has at its heart an empty, almost totalitarian quality.

Cool in Politics

Having conquered popular culture, the final step must be for Cool to invade politics. Following the collapse of the ideologies of the left – from Soviet communism and Trotskyism, through new left Marxism to democratic socialism – a whole generation of young people in the UK finds great difficulty engaging in politics because current politics contains nothing to engage them. Faced with politics seminars from college lecturers whose beliefs were formed during the ill-fated renaissance of proletarian struggle in the early '70s (the miners' strike, the 'three day week'), while simultaneously harassed by the threat of unemployment and benefit cuts, their beleaguered state of mind stands comparison with those disillusioned GIs and never-illusioned black-Americans who invented Cool in the first place.

That perhaps is why there is such a strong revival of interest in everything to do with the '60s counter-culture, which may have arisen spontaneously among the music-loving young but is currently being fanned by the style press, including the broadsheet daily newspapers, and television. However, the version of the '60s that the press so obsessively rehashes is a curiously apolitical one, and one could easily forget that at the heart of the counter-culture lay an instinctive revulsion against the fundamental assumptions of consumerism: money was not to be allowed to be the measure of all things; mere products (even drugs) could never bring happiness; culture should not be subordinated to the needs of business; ownership of goods is a fool's paradise, and so on. What bound together the groupuscules of radical students, underground newspaper collectives and cultural crazies in the '60s was a curious composite material woven from Cool and anti-capitalist politics. This contradiction did not go entirely unnoticed at the time, but the prevailing enthusiasm was sufficient to keep things from flying apart for a while. In the '90s re-run, the media have unpicked this rough material and extracted certain threads (obsession with personal appearance, fashion and irony) and thrown away the radical debris.

Cool is never directly political, and politics, almost by definition, can never be Cool. To get anywhere in politics you need to care passionately about something, whether it is a cause or merely the achievement of personal power, and you need to sacrifice present pleasures to the long and tedious process of campaigning and party organization. Nor has any party yet, outside of the lunatic fringe, proclaimed the pursuit of Cool as its election platform – such a platform would presumably have to include legalizing all drugs, abolishing all taxes and yet simultaneously paying generous unemployment benefits, which might make life tricky for the first Cool treasurer.

Nevertheless, Cool has deep implications for politics and politicians. We have already referred to Mark Lilla's observations on the contradiction between right-wing economics and left-wing social attitudes in the USA, and offered Cool as the solution to the dilemma he posed. Not only is Cool apolitical but it actively tends to dissolve the categories of left and right, by decoupling economic and social assumptions that have been more or less fixed since the French Revolution. Left has almost always stood for a combination of liberal social policies and state intervention in economics, whereas right has always stood for conservative social policies and laissez-faire economics. Cool overthrows these assumptions by embracing both economic and social laissez-faire, sharing the far right's distrust of governmental spying and meddling, but not their moralism or 'family values'. Cool is by preference apolitical, but if forced to take sides will usually side with the more libertarian option, which may be on the left or right in different historical contexts. There is a sense in which Cool is the inverse of Fascism, which embraces precisely the opposite combination – repressively conservative social policies with corporatist economics. For its part, the Christian right has always recognized Cool as its sworn enemy (or the Antichrist if you will) from the earliest days in the '50s when it railed against the 'jungle music' perverting the youth of the nation, and smashed rock 'n' roll records on television.

In the context of US politics this is of vital importance because it makes the Cool generations the pivotal sector capable of keeping the Democrats in power, since the decline or defection of the white working classes. It is no coincidence that there have only been two truly Cool US presidents, Kennedy and Clinton – both were Democrats, and both effectively harnessed the youth vote. If you doubt that Kennedy was Cool, then stop looking at his policies (except perhaps on Civil Rights) and look instead at the haircut, the smile – and the clandestine sexual liaisons.

Kennedy's term was perhaps the last time that US youth was fully engaged by official (as opposed to fringe) party politics and his assassination, along with Watergate, made a decisive contribution to that dark and paranoid disillusion that still debilitates Cool culture. Cool youth now votes for the Democrats not because it likes them, but because it detests the moralizing Christian right more. If evidence for this assertion is needed, the American public's reaction to the Monica Lewinsky affair surely provides it: what they told pollsters was that they didn't respect Clinton much (although they didn't think his peccadillo that important), but they *feared* the Special Prosecutor, Kenneth Starr, and despised his informant, Linda Tripp.

The same logic holds true in the UK, and probably in most European countries: Cool youth is unlikely to be actively mobilized in the cause of any sort of traditional socialism, even of the most democratic varieties, but it is nevertheless fiercely opposed to any talk of moral regeneration and family values, and that will pose increasing problems for all right-wing conservative parties. In the UK, perhaps it was a coincidence that the 1997 return of the first Labour Government in eighteen years should coincide with a revival of '60s fashions, music and drug consumption among young people – but then again, perhaps not. Having a Prime Minister who owned a Fender Stratocaster and who invites pop stars to tea (in the '60s Labour Prime Minister Harold Wilson invited The Beatles to breakfast) persuaded the UK press to label Tony Blair's New Labour Government 'Cool Britannia' (and the fact that they may have stolen the phrase from a flavour of Ben & Jerry's American ice cream is almost too good to be true as regards our argument). Although Blair has disclaimed the title when asked directly, there is a sense in which embracing Cool would fit his purposes, at least on one level.

The Blair Government embarked on a more radical programme of reform of British institutions than many expected, but it is a programme that seeks to cut out dead wood from both the left and the right: welfare dependency as well as hereditary peers, entrenched anti-business attitudes as well as social exclusion. To the extent that the New Labour project involves demolishing the legacy of the Second World War and the post-war consensus, Cool might seem to be an appropriate 'branding' for the party. Certainly the Conservatives appear to think so: the main priority for Conservative strategists is not currently to produce vote-winning policies, but to rebrand themselves as the 'Naturally Cool Party'. This is not *quite* as daft as it sounds, since a Conservative Party with softened social policies might be able to attack New Labour from a libertarian direction – perhaps even by promising to legalize drugs, although we wish lots of luck to the person who first tries that out on the ladies of the Conservative Conference.

There is, however, a more serious problem for politicians who attempt to harness the energy of UK youth culture under the banner of Cool. The main planks of the New Labour project are to restore our disintegrating sense of community (by shoring up the traditional family and eliminating drug abuse), to halt the rise of crime and to improve the performance of our education system. But Cool stands for almost exactly the opposite values: it is intrinsically anti-family, pro-drug, anti-authority and admires criminality (it is more than coincidence that criminals say 'he's cool' to indicate that someone is one of them). What's more, ironic detachment is a poor adhesive for any society as well as being extremely difficult to harness to any sort of collective endeavour. The plain fact is that the Cool attitude is an obstacle to several of the more important goals of New Labour's programme: the promotion of work, school and family, and the reduction of violent crime and drug abuse.

Cool retains all its traditional fondness for drugs, spanning the full range from weed and magic mushrooms, through speed, ecstasy and cocaine, to the still fashionable 'junkie chic'. Heroin abuse is on a steep increase today, and among ever-younger age groups. The most heart-breaking news stories of 1999 concerned the overdose of a twelve-year-old heroin addict in Glasgow, and the scarcely believable revelation that the highest per-capita-rate of heroin addiction in the UK is to be found in Fraserburgh, a fishing village in the north of Scotland, among *trawler crews*. The consequences of drug abuse are strongly affected by economic and social class, so that while a heroin habit might present a severe inconvenience to a London socialite, it is often terminal for kids on a housing project in Leeds or Chicago, for whom jail or the mortuary are the most probable destinations. A triumph of Cool means living permanently with the negative effects of both drug abuse and the penal policies that governments apply in pursuing their futile 'war on drugs'. Among black US youth one-in-six passes through the jail system and a gunshot wound has become the prime cause of death.

So can New Labour recapture young people's hearts and minds without fatally compromising key parts of its programme? It is unlikely that Labour would want (or could afford) to buy their affections by restoring lost unemployment benefits, and the party is equally unlikely to compromise on, say, legalizing cannabis. The only remaining possibility is to discover some 'big idea' that could make caring Cool, but that is almost an oxymoron. Blair's project needs to haul young minds back from the more nihilistic and destructive aspects of Cool, but it is hard to see where it can obtain the traction – trying to encompass Cool within a moralizing, Christian socialist framework may prove too much even for a 'spin-master' of Blair's undoubted abilities. Cool is the philosophy of Hollywood's 'new aristocracy', not of the Labour Party activist. Far from being a friend to social democracy, Cool may prove to be its grave-digger.

Global Cooling

Some might argue that Cool is primarily a Western phenomenon, and that elsewhere in the world there are other equally powerful forces, for example militant Islam, that will check its progress. Another possibility is that in non-Christian cultures the Cool pose does not offer the same attraction that it does in Western societies – there is, for example, no equivalent expression in the Chinese language. The people of the African continent, the original birthplace of Cool, are embroiled in a seemingly never-ending succession of civil wars. Is Russia perhaps too broke (or too cold) to enjoy being Cool?

Actually we do not believe in any of these counter-arguments. Wherever the standard of living rises to a point where television, pop music and the Hollywood movie are available (and that leaves out very few areas of the globe now) then young people will both recognize and culti-vate Cool. What Cool now represents is the influence of the free market in personal relationships and sexuality, and whether politicians like it or not, it is likely that the majority of the younger generation throughout the world now aspire to this degree of freedom. What's more, they are unlikely to be gainsaid by mere moralizing, and it takes a dictatorship, or the mili-tary triumph of religious fundamentalism, to divert them from its pursuit.

Cool even flourished as a dissident force under Soviet communism, where Western popular culture was prohibited and could only be seen via the black market: throughout Eastern Europe a Cool pose was recog-nized as a mark of passive resistance to communism. It is at least arguable that Cool helped eventually to bring down communism, as it represents precisely those 'decadent Western values' that the regime sought to exclude – the black market in Beatles' albums and Levi jeans is what lost the hearts and minds of the whole post-war generation for communism. In 1989 East German youths hoisted the MTV flag over the Berlin Wall as it was being pulled down.

So is Cool then destined to rule the world? To ask this is the same as to ask whether consumer capitalism and parliamentary democracy are destined to rule the world, because if they do then Cool will surely follow. Francis Fukuyama's *End of History* notwithstanding, that is by no means yet a certainty. The 1998 economic crisis in the Far East demonstrated that capitalism is still an unstable and unpredictable system, prone to boom and bust when least expected. Since the collapse of communism there may be no major political movement offering any alternative to capitalism, but there is serious opposition to legal, global capitalism from the equally global world of organized crime. The manufacture and sale of illegal drugs now rates among the top five worldwide industries by turnover, and in several countries, including Colombia, Thailand and Jamaica, drug gangs are sufficiently powerful to be perceived as a threat by the legitimate governments – rule by drug barons and warlords, although anachronistic, is by no means inconceivable. Cool has always been fascinated by gangsterdom – indeed has been the approved attitude of gangsters – and the mass-market popularity of gangsta rap and movies like *Goodfellas* suggests that nothing has changed in that respect. In short, Cool has a dangerously ambivalent attitude toward the rule of law and could accommodate criminal neo-feudalism just as well as it does consumer capitalism. The uncomfortable truth is that, compared to the excitements of the drug and gun culture, a prosperous, well-ordered society is boring. Fukuyama takes a rather Panglossian approach to such matters: so far as Cool is concerned history isn't just over, it is the ultimate negative, something that is washed up, finished with, as in, 'Bang! You're history.'

So how bad could it be if Cool did rule the world? Certainly, with capitalism unleashed and unregulated the traditional left would experience an absolute defeat. Cool consumer capitalism has discovered, as Thomas Frank puts it, how to construct cultural machines that transform alienation and despair into consent. But the triumph of Cool would be no more comforting to those on the traditional right since it represents the collapse of all their most cherished values. The USA, as Mark Lilla's question makes clear, must be our model for what happens when a society embraces the free market both in labour and leisure, while losing interest in party politics: unprecedented prosperity for the many; misery for the few; Wall Street at an all-time high; jails overflowing and a lack of any truly oppositional (as opposed to knee-jerk reactionary) politics. The maintenance of a healthy democracy requires a perceptible difference between the parties of left and right, and real confrontations over real issues, and in this light the emergence of an apolitical Cool generation is alarming.

Cool prefers the image of rebellion, as offered by glamorous terrorists, gangsters and wasted rock musicians, to the hard, boring slog of real politics, and we would all do well to remember that Adolf Hitler was also a cultural rebel with artistic pretensions, a distinctive haircut, big trousers and kinky boots. And sure enough, in February 1999 James Brown (founder of *Loaded* magazine, the bible of Cool 'lad culture'), was asked to resign as editor of *GQ* magazine after publishing an article that named the Nazis, and Field Marshal Rommel in particular, among 'the sharpest men of the century'. Not evil, just plain silly.

Cool may once have been an expression of rebellion but it is surely not any longer. The real question is whether or not it can sustain the key elements, the rule of law and freedom of conscience, that make Western democracy the least bad form of government ever invented. The picture is murky and contradictory: on the one hand Cool values personal freedom above all; it hates racism; it is egalitarian and hedonistic in temperament. On the other hand, it is fascinated by violence, drugs and criminality and mesmerized by the sight of naked power. But this book is not an effort to predict the future, rather to explain the past – to make visible the ambiguous influence of Cool in modern life precisely so that people might start to debate such matters, and more seriously weigh the pros and cons of boredom versus excitement, order versus turmoil, tolerance versus thuggery. In the end we shall, as ever, have to wait and see what happens, for deprived of Marxism's historic inevitability the future's not ours to see . . . 'que sera, sera' (Sly Stone's version of course, not Doris Day's).

Cool values personal freedom above all, hates racism, is egalitarian and hedonistic in temperament, but is fascinated with violence, drugs and criminality . . . It remains to be seen how far it values the rule of law and freedom of conscience, which underpin Western democracy.

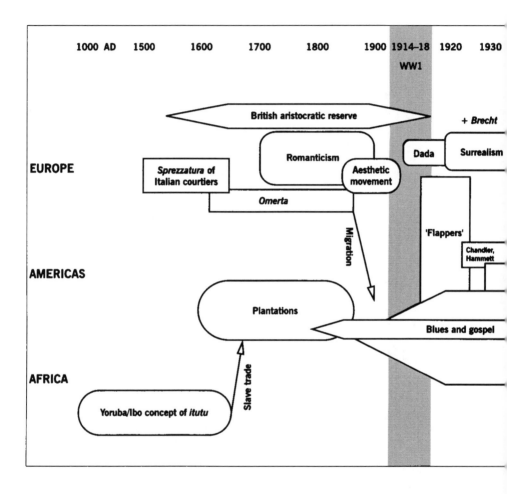

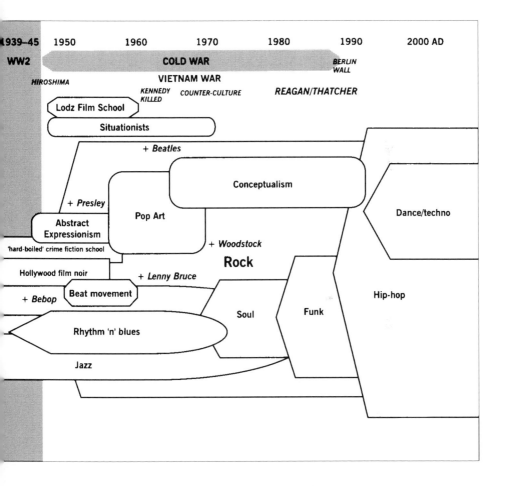

1939–45   1950   1960   1970   1980   1990   2000 AD

WW2   COLD WAR   BERLIN
                                                             WALL

HIROSHIMA   VIETNAM WAR

                     KENNEDY   COUNTER-CULTURE   REAGAN/THATCHER
                     KILLED

Lodz Film School

Situationists

+ Beatles

                                    Conceptualism

+ Presley
                  Pop Art   Dance/techno

Abstract
Expressionism

'hard-boiled' crime fiction school   + Woodstock

Hollywood film noir   + Lenny Bruce   Rock

+ Bebop   Beat movement   Hip-hop

                                        Soul   Funk

Rhythm 'n' blues

Jazz

References

Introduction

1 Norman Mailer, 'The White Negro', *Advertisements for Myself* (Cambridge, MA, 1992), p. 352.

2 Thomas Frank, *The Conquest of Cool* (Chicago, 1997), p. 17.

3 Marcel Tadesi, *Cool: The Signs and Meanings of Adolescence* (Toronto, 1994), p. 1.

4 Frank, *The Conquest of Cool*, p. 43.

5 Thom Gunn, 'Elvis Presley', in A. Alvarez, ed., *The New Poetry* (Harmondsworth, 1962), p. 136.

One: What Is Cool?

1 Mark Irving and Marcus Field, *Lofts* (London, 1999).

2 Desmond Christy, *The Guardian*, 3 July 1999.

3 Jonathon Green, *Dictionary of Slang* (London, 1998).

4 Peter N. Stearns, *American Cool: Constructing a Twentieth Century Emotional Style* (New York, 1994), p. 1.

5 *Ibid.*

6 Marcel Tadesi, *Cool: The Signs and Meanings of Adolescence* (Toronto, 1994), p. 37.

Two: Out of Africa

1 Peter N. Stearns, *American Cool: Constructing a Twentieth Century Emotional Style* (New York, 1994), p. 1.

2 Robert Farris Thompson, *African Art in Motion* (New York, 1979), p. 43.

3 Robert Farris Thompson, *Flash of the Spirit* (New York, 1984), p. 11.

4 Trevor Verryn, D. Chidester *et al.*, eds, *African Traditional Religion in South Africa* (Westport, 1998), p. 368.

5 Gerald Suttles, cited in Thompson, *African Art in Motion*, p. 45.

6 Richard Majors and Janet Mancini Billson, *Cool Pose: The Dilemmas of Black Manhood in America* (New York, 1992), p. 57.

7 Edmund S. Morgan, 'The Big American Crime', *New York Review of Books*, XLV/19, 3 December 1998, pp. 14–18.

8 Orlando Patterson, *Rituals of Blood: Consequences of Slavery in Two American Centuries* (New York, 1999), p. 213.

9 Richard Wright, *Black Power* (New York, 1954).

10 Langston Hughes, quoted in Majors and Mancini Billson, *Cool Pose*, p. 1.

11 Thompson, *African Art in Motion*, p. 45.

12 Richard Wright, in Paul Oliver, *Blues Fell this Morning* (Cambridge, 1960), p. xiv.

13 *Ibid.*

14 Greil Marcus, *Mystery Train* (New York, 1974), p. 22.

15 Richard Wright, in Oliver, *Blues Fell this Morning*, p. xv.

16 Richard Cook and Brian Morton, *The Penguin Guide to Jazz on CD* (London, 1998), p. 381.

17 James Lincoln Collier, *Jazz: The American Theme Song* (New York and Oxford, 1993), p. 143–4.

18 David Rosenthal, *Hard Bop: Jazz and Black Music 1955–1965* (Oxford, 1992), p. 23.

19 Marcus, *Mystery Train*, p. 6.

20 *Ibid.*, p. 122.

Three: A Whiter Shade of Cool

1 Robert Farris Thompson, *African Art in Motion* (New York, 1979), p. 43.

2 Richard Lanham, *A Handlist of Rhetorical Terms* (California, 1991).

3 See John Harvey, *Men in Black* (London, 1995).

4 Will Hutton, 'The war that changed the world', *The Observer*, 8 November 1998, p. 14.

5 Paul Fussell, *The Great War and Modern Memory* (Oxford, 1975), p. 24.

6 Peter N. Stearns, *American Cool: Constructing a Twentieth Century Emotional Style* (New York, 1994), p. 231.

7 'Concerning Poor BB', *Bertholt Brecht: Selected Poems*, ed. and trans. H. R. Hays (New York, 1959), p. 15.

8 *Ibid*., p. 165.

9 *Ibid*., p. 147.

10 Stearns, *American Cool*, p. 231.

11 Herbert Gold, *Bohemia: Digging the Roots of Cool* (New York, 1993), p. 43.

12 Quoted in David Halberstam, *The Fifties* (New York, 1993), p. 299.

13 James Park Sloan, *Jerzy Kosinski* (New York, 1996), pp. 67–8, p. 9.

14 'Adorno/ Marcuse Letters 1969', *New Left Review*, CCXXX (1999), p. 132.

15 Sloan, *Jerzy Kosinski*, p. 67.

16 Norman Mailer, 'The White Negro', *Advertisements for Myself* (Cambridge, MA, 1992), p. 340.

17 Jack Kerouac, *Some of the Dharma* (New York, 1999), p. 63.

18 *Ibid*.

19 Mailer, 'The White Negro', p. 339.

Four: That's Cool Too . . .

1 Peter Biskind, *Easy Riders, Raging Bulls* (London, 1998), p. 49.

2 *Ibid*., p. 84.

3 *Ibid*., p. 83.

4 Guy Debord, *Panegyric* (Paris, 1989), p. 7.

5 Ross McKibbin, *Classes and Cultures: England 1918–53* (Oxford, 1998), p. 408.

Five: Cool Cracks Up

1 Norman Mailer, 'The White Negro', *Advertisements for Myself* (Cambridge, MA, 1992), p. 342.

2 Gordon Burn, *Happy Like Murderers* (London, 1998), p. 187.

3 Richard Benson, *Arena* (March 1999), p. 78.

Six: The Look of Cool

1 Margaret Olin, 'Gaze', *Critical Terms for Art History*, R. Nelson and R. Schiff, eds. (Chicago, 1996), p. 209.

2 Bice Curiger, *Birth of the Cool: American Painting from Georgia O'Keeffe to Christopher Wool*, exh. cat., Kunsthaus Zurich (Zurich, 1997), p. 9.

3 David Sylvester, *About Modern Art* (London, 1997), p. 389.

4 *Ibid.*, p. 388.

5 *Ibid.*

Seven: Cool Relations

1 Peter Biskind, *Easy Riders, Raging Bulls* (London, 1998), p. 174.

2 Anna and Robert Francoeur, *Hot & Cool Sex: Cultures in Conflict* (Los Angeles, 1974), p. 39.

3 *Ibid.*, p. 37.

4 Kenneth Tynan, 'In Memory of Mr. Coward', *Sound of Two Hands Clapping* (London, 1975), p. 58.

5 Susan Sontag, note 56 of 'Notes on Camp', collected in *A Susan Sontag Reader* (New York, 1983), p. 119.

Eight: Cool Psyche

1 Adam Phillips, *On Kissing, Tickling and Being Bored* (London, 1994), pp. 43–4.

2 Richard Majors and Janet Mancini Billson, *Cool Pose: The Dilemmas of Black Manhood in America* (New York, 1992), p. 8.

3 Ian Buruma, 'Joys and Perils of Victimhood', *New York Review of Books*, 8 April 1999.

Nine: Cool Rules

1 Peter N. Stearns, *American Cool: Constructing a Twentieth Century Emotional Style* (New York, 1994), p. 231.

2 *The London Evening Standard*, 15 February 1999, p. 25.

3 Mark Lilla, 'A Tale of Two Reactions', *New York Review of Books*, 14 May 1998.

4 *Ibid*.

5 Stearns, *American Cool*, p. 156.

6 Studs Terkel, *Working* (Chicago, 1972), p. 1.

7 Thomas Frank, *The Conquest of Cool* (Chicago, 1997), p. 26.

8 *Conversations with Anthony Giddens* (London, 1998), p. 31.

9 Don DeLillo, *Underworld* (London, 1998), p. 109.

10 Guy Debord, *The Society of the Spectacle*, trans. Donald Nicholson Smith (New York, 1994), p. 44.

11 Marcel Tadesi, *Cool: The Signs and Meanings of Adolescence* (Toronto, 1994), p. 128.

Acknowledgements

We would like to thank John Lea and Mark Antliff for their critical advice and encouragement at the beginning of this project when we needed it most. We are also very grateful to Mick Gold, David Downes, Nina Fishman and Marion Hills for reading the manuscript and providing many helpful insights. Thanks are also due to Simon Frazer, Peter Ansorge, Gill Perry, Anna Gruetzner Robins, Teresa Gleadowe, Phil McManus, Nicholas Jacobs and Michael Coveney for steering us in the direction of some important material. Many thanks to Jane Ferrett for her assistance with the picture research. Finally, thanks to the Pineapple, where the idea was born and nurtured.

Photographic Acknowledgements

The authors and publishers wish to express their thanks to the following sources of illustrative material and/or permission to reproduce it:

The Advertising Archives: pp. 17, 168; Associated Press/James Fasuekoi: p. 37; Glenn A. Baker Archives: p. 50; Barnaby's Picture Library: pp. 18, 20, 63, 64, 73, 82, 83, 86, 98, 116, 117, 119, 130 (top), 133, 143, 150, 154, 157; © Bettmann/Corbis: pp. 27, 106; K. J. Eddy: p. 154; *Folio* magazine, 1999: p. 163; Brian Gibbs: p. 157; © Lynn Goldsmith/Corbis: p. 110; William Gottlieb: p. 47; Ronald Grant Archives: pp. 66, 135; Lesley Howling: pp. 130 (top), 150; © Hulton-Deutsch Collection/Corbis: p. 124; *Internationale Situationniste*: p. 89; Graham Keen: p. 67; Lisa Law: p. 14; The Marlborough Gallery, Inc., New York (© Alex Katz: *Round Hill*, 1977, oil on canvas): p. 152; Musée d'Orsay, Paris: p. 115; Musée du Louvre, Paris: p. 54; The National Portrait Gallery, Smithsonian Institution, Washington, DC (gift of W. Tjark Weiss, in memory of his father, Winold Weiss): p. 41; Michael Ochs Archives: p. 137; Collection of Dick Pountain: pp. 88, 89; © Eldad Rafaeli/Corbis: p. 179 (top); Mikki Rain: p. 100;